THE CITY OF COVENTRY
— Images —
From the Past

THE CITY OF COVENTRY

Images
From the Past

David McGrory

JONES - SANDS PUBLISHING

First Published in Great Britain by
Jones-Sands Publishing 1996

ISBN 0-947764-91-7

To preserve the quality and character, the pictures in this publication
have not been retouched in any way.

This book was designed by:-

Jones-Sands Publishing
Upton
Wirral
L49 6PQ
England
Tele/Fax (0151 606 0240)

Typeset in Great Britain by Jones-Sands Publishing
Printed by Clifford Press Ltd, Coventry
Marketed and distributed by Jones-Sands Publishing

AUTHOR'S ACKNOWLEDGEMENTS

Many thanks to the following for without them this book.would not have been possible:

Coventry City Council, Roger Vaughan (City Archivist), Coventry Local Studies and Andrew Mealey;
Albert Peck (Methodist Central Hall Archivist); John Ashby, Ina Harrison, Roger Bailey, Trevor Pring,
Cliff Barlow, Eric Whitehead, Dennis Beasley, James Armer, William Gibbons, Lucy Bromwich and
Richard Sands.

DEDICATION

For my Heather with love.

Illustrations:

Page 1: An 1860s engraving looking south up Great Butcher Row
Page 2: Looking towards the great east window of St. Michael's around 1920
Page 3: Looking down Priory Row in 1926

FOREWORD

For Coventrians born and bred, it is certain that this work will appeal as a rare and comprehensive example of the true spirit and cherished values of Coventry and Coventrians. If the rich and illustrious past of a thousand and more years is not about Coventrians then it is nothing.

From the past came engineering and trade excellence and a patent gaiety that typifies Coventry folk throughout the ages together with a pioneering and visionary approach that has sought to accommodate a cosmopolitan population that continues to live in harmony with each other and enriches the character that is the quintessential Midlander and Coventrian.

My own memories of Coventry, dating from the early thirties, consist in part of walking to Cheylesmore School (now Elm Bank) via Freeth Street, Jordan Well, Much Park Street, St. John's Street and Mile Lane and therefore enjoying a nodding acquaintance with much of old Coventry. On November 14th 1940 I can recall being under the old St. Michael's Cathedral Crypt which had been converted into an air raid shelter and afforded a great sense of protection until the conflagration that destroyed it.

Coventry has thus seen change through not only social and industrial decay but through severe aerial bombardment that consequently led to the change in physical shape – particularly to the city centre. However, Coventry has always been able to 'digest' such transition and remain responsive to the needs of Coventrians. It has grown to be a unique centre of international reconciliation by means of our wonderful cathedral, built to the glory of God, and leads the world in these studies. During my own electoral lifetime, I have seen Coventry as a city with no university to one with two of the very finest and increasingly respected; University of Warwick (that has its origins in Coventry) and Coventry University itself.

Coventry is therefore both an ancient city and a place of vision for the future. At the time of this publication, the City is in the process of assembling a Millennium Bid that will allow us to celebrate the last 1,000 plus years and bequeath a fine future heritage of which we can all be proud. Today Coventry is "on the up", embracing new challenges, trade diversification and "high tech" companies where we once had primarily the motor car industry, the Centenary of which is also being currently celebrated as Coventry was the place where it all began and where Coventry's new industrial landscape bears a monument to this tradition.

We shall be limited only by our own aspirations in Coventry. In the past, security has equalled ability, the ability to produce skills and industrial organisation that has benefited the majority. There is a tremendous reservoir of skill and facility for various updating of qualification and I am delighted to be invited to write this introductory message which is that from our beginnings shall we know our destinies.

Councillor Stan Hodson July 1996
Lord Mayor

INTRODUCTION

The origins of Coventry are lost in the mist of time but clues point to the fact that there was probably an ancient track crossing the site in very early times. The track, known to the Romans, crossed through the centre north to south heading for Baginton and beyond. Other clues from surviving traditions also suggest that Coventry may have been a sacred site; legends relate to the Celtic-Roman water goddess, Coventina and rituals associated with sacred wells, pools and tree's (i.e. Cofa's Tree). Even our own Godiva legend has pagan origins associated with a yearly fertility ritual involving a goddess on horseback, making it in many ways more fascinating than the present legend.

With all this going on it is not surprising that around the year 700 A.D. a convent was founded here attached to the settlement led by Osburg (Osburga) who later became a saint. In 1043 Earl Leofric and Lady Godiva founded the church and Benedictine monastery of St. Mary. This drew commerce to Coventry and the settlement officially became a city when the Bishop moved here in 1095, thus creating the Cathedral and Priory of St. Mary. The Priory became one of the richest in the land and thrived until the monks were evicted in 1539 during the Dissolution .

The city wall, begun in 1355, made the city a central stronghold and a target for Charles I on the outbreak of the Civil War in 1642. The King hoped to make the city his seat of war but after demanding entrance with his army by force of arms he was repulsed by Parliamentarian forces. On hearing that Lord Brooke was heading for the city with an army, the King made a tactical withdrawal and headed straight for Nottingham where he raised his standard. Due to this incident, after the Restoration Charles II ordered that the city walls be raised to the ground. This work was carried out by the Earl of Northampton and 500 troops in July 1662.

The 18th century was a settled period for the city and it prospered from its well-established wool and dyeing trade. Silk weaving was also introduced and the city, already famous for its 'True as Coventry Blue' dye, produced silk in all the colours of the rainbow. Another new mechanically based industry was the introduction of clock making. This would grow into a massive watch making industry which along with the weaving industry collapsed in 1861, bringing much hardship to the city and mass migration.

(Left) This mid-nineteenth century engraving shows Broadgate looking towards Cross Cheaping as it would have looked in the 18th century. Once all Coventry's Streets looked like this lined with ancient timbered houses, some dating back to the 14th century.

Within a few years migration out of the city turned to migration into the city as the sewing machine industry, founded by Starley and Turner, slowly turned into the cycle industry making Coventry the largest producer of cycles in the world. The production of cycles naturally led to the manufacture of the motor car that began with the floatation of the Daimler Company in 1896. The first British built motor car left the company's shared factory known as 'Motor Mills' in Drapers Field, Radford in 1897.

In times of war Coventry's factories turned to armaments production and not surprisingly the city was targeted by the gentlemen of the Luftwaffe. Coventry suffered many raids but none could compare with the mass bombing of high explosives and incendiaries that consumed the heart of the city for eleven long hours beginning on the evening of November 14th 1940. This and further raids on the city left 1,200 dead and 1,746 injured.

The heart of Coventry lay flattened and no sooner was the rubble cleared when plans were being made for its rebuilding. Donald Gibson was engaged as city architect and he produced a revolutionary plan for the city. This began with the making of Broadgate into a garden island that was opened by the Princess Elizabeth in 1948. Soon after, work began on the Upper Precinct starting with Broadgate House which was opened in 1953. By 1955 the Upper Precinct was complete and Gibson left. His work was carried on by his successor Arthur Ling who completed the Lower Precinct, Smithford Way and Market Way. The rebuilding of the centre was completed by Terrance Gregory and in reality has never ended to this day.

Coventry is an extraordinary city and in some ways an unfortunate city for few can claim to have lost two cathedral's and enough timbered buildings by bomb and bulldozer to make a small town. Coventry's population is extraordinary for it is made up of people from Ireland, Scotland, Wales, Asia, and every county in England. Few can actually trace their families back here more than two or three generations. With this mix comes some of the finest skills in the land, skills that once made the city a boom town. Coventry now is in a stage of transition for almost all its industrial base has gone and is slowly being replaced by office based work.

Coventry is changing as it has throughout its history, modern changes have been drastic and sometimes shocking. Within the pages that follow you will witness many, many extraordinary changes that have made the City of Coventry what it is today.

David McGrory
1996

BEGINNINGS

This sketch based on that of William Smyth in 1576 is probably the oldest view in existence of the walled city of Coventry. Smyth (or Smith) was Rouge Dragon Pursuivant Herald to Queen Elizabeth I and drew this sketch, one of many, while compiling his book *A Particular Description of England*.

The wall you see was begun in 1355 when the Mayor Richard Stoke laid the foundation stone at New

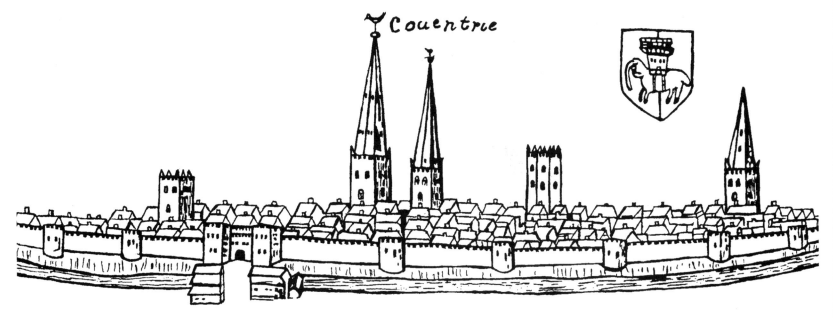

Gate by Whitefriars. The view is from the northeast and shows a much bigger Cook Street Gate entered via a moated bridge. The towers from right to left are Greyfriars (later Christchurch); the double towered entrance to the great priory of Coventry, St. Mary's, some of which still stands off Trinity Street. Next we see Holy Trinity, St. Michael's and lastly not St. John's (that would be off the picture far right) but the church of the Friary of Whitefriars.

This huge church, which was cruciform in shape, stretched a massive 303 feet in length (the old Cathedral is 240 ft) and like the priory and Greyfriars fell at the Dissolution and was sold by the Crown to the Corporation in 1539. In 1572 the Corporation had most of the main building demolished leaving the tower and its spire standing. In 1574 the spire was encouraged to fall leaving a forlorn tower standing alone and this is what Smyth sketched two years later.

All that remains of this great church is a few fine medieval choir stalls in Holy Trinity church and the old Grammar School in Hales Street.

'The ground plott of Coventre' as mapped by John Speed in 1610. This represents the basic bones of the city laid down in medieval times. Surprisingly, Coventry of the late 19th century was not much bigger, due to much of the building being centred on infilling in courts and gardens. Many of the street-names are still identifiable today, others have to be pointed out like St. John's Bridges whose earlier name was Inter Pontes, a latin name meaning between bridges as two bridges had to be crossed in this street. We know it now as simply the Burges. This name may have developed from the regional pronunciation of the word "burge," meaning bridge.

Another name of interest is Dogge Lane, this led into an area called the 'Dogge Londe' and on into Upper and Lower Shuckmoor (from the Anglo-saxon, 'succa' meaning demon = Demon's Moor) in Radford.

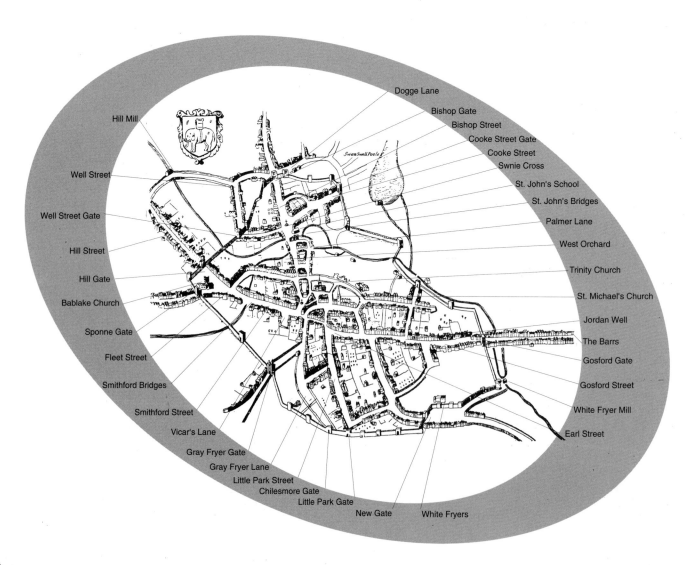

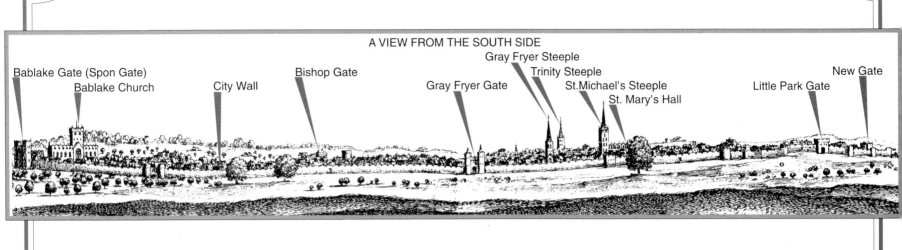

A VIEW FROM THE SOUTH SIDE

Bablake Gate (Spon Gate)
Bablake Church
City Wall
Bishop Gate
Gray Fryer Gate
Gray Fryer Steeple
Trinity Steeple
St.Michael's Steeple
St. Mary's Hall
Little Park Gate
New Gate

North and South prospects of walled Coventry drawn by Wenceslaus Hollar around 1655 for Sir William Dugdale's *Antiquities of Warwickshire* (1656). This is the Coventry of the 17th century, the Civil War had ended a few years earlier and Cromwell was Lord Protector of the Commonwealth.

This is the last picture of walled Coventry for seven years later, on 22 July 1662 the Earl of Northampton led 500 troops in the destruction of the massive city wall. The order was given by Charles II because in August 1642 the wall had stopped his father from making Coventry his wartime capital during the English Civil War. Northampton is said to have been ordered to slight the walls but instead overstepped his orders by literally demolishing the whole thing.

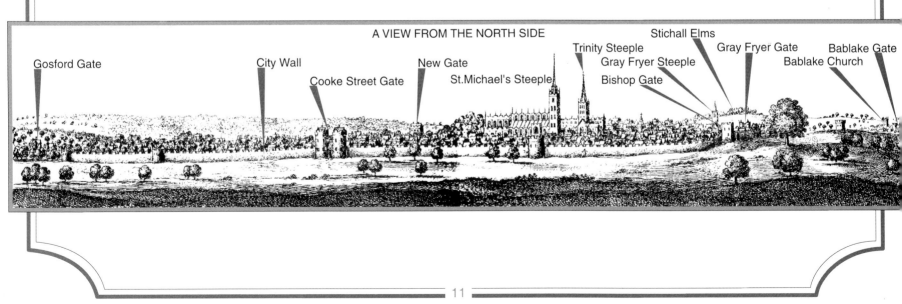

A VIEW FROM THE NORTH SIDE

Gosford Gate
City Wall
Cooke Street Gate
New Gate
St.Michael's Steeple
Trinity Steeple
Stichall Elms
Gray Fryer Steeple
Bishop Gate
Gray Fryer Gate
Bablake Gate
Bablake Church

(*Left*) A detailed print of 1888 giving artist G.R. Webster's fairly accurate idea of how mid-eighteenth century Broadgate and Cross Cheaping looked. In the centre stands the once famed Coventry Cross, the second such cross to stand in Cross Cheaping (Cheaping meaning market).

Work on this magnificent cross began in 1541 after Sir William Hollis, Mayor of London (son of a Coventrian) left two hundred pounds for its erection. It was completed in 1543 and reached a height of 57 feet. The cross was decorated with images of kings and saints and was painted in bright colours and smothered in gold leaf. In fact it held so much gold that on a sunny day it literally glowed. The cross soon grew famed throughout England and the well known rhyme 'Ride a cock horse to Banbury Cross' is thought to have originally referred to Coventry Cross. The cross stood until 1771 when it was dismantled and parts of it were spread throughout the county.

Coventry in the 18th century was a prosperous city; its wealth based on the fruit of the loom. The coach in the print was a regular sight in the city for such vehicles sped to London, Liverpool, and Leicester, to mention but a few. The King's Head in Smithford Street for example ran coaches every evening at 11.30 pm to reach London at 4.00 pm the following day.

The Father of Methodism, John Wesley wrote in his journal in 1779 after preaching in the city, 'I took coach for London. I was nobly attended; behind the coach were ten convicted felons, loudly blaspheming and rattling on their chains; by my side sat a man with a loaded blunderbuss, and another upon the coach.'

After the Dissolution Sir Ralph Sadler acquired the grange and sold it on to John Hales of Whitefriars in 1548. After John Hales' death his estate was passed on to his brothers eldest son also called John Hales. This John Hales, wishing to leave Whitefriars for a country residence, demolished the old grange and just in front of its moated site built a superb mansion; completed in 1586 he called it 'New House.'

The house passed through various hands including Sir Richard Burnaby, Sir Christopher Yelverton; the Strode family who all mysteriously died within a short time of their occupancy and into the 1720's the Bohun family, many of whom's members represented the city in Parliament. In its heyday the New House was indeed a fine building domed and turreted it had over one hundred and fifty windows which overlooked seven walled gardens intersected with paths and decorated with classical statues. It was placed so the occupants would have fine views of the countryside and the three spires of Coventry.

After its demolition all that remained was the Keresley Road entrance formed by two stone pillars surmounted by stone balls. Later in the 19th century another house was built on the site called the 'Moat House.' This building was added to over the years by some of the city most respectable citizens and remained in use into the 1920's when it too was demolished for the building of a new housing estate. The last thing to fall was the old 'New House' gate which had stood for 340 years. The site is now houses and a block of flats and no-one would ever know that the 'New House' ever existed.

(*Above*) This was once considered one of the finest houses in England. The engraving is of the New House, Keresley as it appeared before its demolition in 1779. The building which stood on the corner of the present Keresley Road and Sadler Road was built on the site of an early 15th century monastic moated grange which belonged to Coventry Priory and was attached to a 436 acre ditched and fenced hunting park, better known as Whitmore Park.

This engraving, published in 1829, shows one of the city's long lost views from what was then known as the Mill Dam. The Mill Dam began life as part of the 'Babbu lacu' a huge lake which ran through the middle of early Coventry.

Over a long period of time this lake naturally silted up leaving smaller pools around the city. One such pool was the Swanswell and the other was the Mill Dam which stretched from beyond Cox Street over to Hales Street. The earliest recorded name for the Mill Dam was St. Osburg's Pool named after the sainted abbess of the nunnery which was built above the pool around the year 700 A.D.

In medieval times the pool was utilised to run the mill attached to the nearby priory; when the dam for this mill was finally removed and the water culverted in the 1840's the pool drained quickly becoming swampy. A few years later drainage work was carried out finally drying the land out and forming what we now know as Pool Meadow.

The buildings in the background are (left to right) St. Michael's, Holy Trinity and the entrance tower of St. Mary's Priory which can still be seen off Trinity Street.

An early 19th century engraving showing the remains of one of the entrance towers to the Benedictine Priory church of St. Mary's. These remains can still been seen off Trinity Street, but what still exists, from about 12 feet up, was rebuilt in 1856 when the Blue Coat School was built.

The Priory of St. Mary, St. Peter, St. Osburg and All Saints was founded on October 4th 1043 by Earl Leofric of Mercia and Lady Godiva, his wife. Within its precincts the great lord and lady stayed on their frequent visits to Coventry.

Inside were housed many relics including the arm of St. Augustine (presented earlier to the nunnery by Canute) and the remains of St. Osburg. Godiva herself took special interest in the church and enriched it with gifts of gold, silver and jewels, so much so that it was said by the chronicler William of Malmesbury 'that the walls seemed too narrow to contain it.'

Later both Godiva and Leofric were laid to rest within this church which, after 1095, became a Cathedral as a Bishops seat was attached to Coventry. The church and precincts were rebuilt in the 13th century in the style of Canterbury, Lichfield and Salisbury, quickly becoming a place of pilgrimage and one of the wealthiest monastic houses in England. The building had a rich and varied history until 1539 when Henry VIII (who had been a recent visitor to the priory) ordered the Dissolution of England's monastic houses. Coventry's cathedral was the only English cathedral to fall and the many monks who served it were put out with no where to go. Coventry was hit badly because Greyfriars, Whitefriars and Charterhouse also fell. The economic impact on the city was disastrous and the population fell from 10,000 to 3,000. The city would never be the same again.

'Remains of the Priory, Coventry' drawn and engraved by Coventry artist David Gee (1793-1872). This section of the precinct of the Priory stood at the bottom of Hill Top and was known as Parliament House. It got its name from the fact that two parliaments were held in the priory in 1404 and 1459 in the Chapter House. As what we see here is only the remains of a wall with a later small building attached, perhaps these ruins did in fact constitute what was earlier the priories Chapter House.

(*Above*) A fine engraving of Cook Street Gate by William Freeman dating around 1805. Cook Street Gate (once also know as Tower Gate) is one of only two gates out of twelve which lined the city wall. In fact the longest remaining piece of wall connects it to Swanswell Gate. The gate was added in the middle of the 15th century to Coventry's two and a half mile long wall, said to be the greatest outside London.

The ditch one can see in the engraving was originally a moat which was flooded in times of trouble. In 1643 the Civil War raged and the ditches were re-cut and connected by new sluices to the Rivers Sherbourne and Albert. The Albert is debateable as a river. Although more of a stream it was always called the Albert or River Albert. By the late 19th century the gate lay derelict and was acquired by Sir William Wyley who presented it to the city in 1913. The gate, which still stands in Cooke Street, was restored in 1918 and 1931.

A fine copper plate etching of Coventry dating around 1860. In this view, seen from fields near the London Road, we see just how close open country was to the city centre. In what was still basically a medieval city, sheep were as common in the city as they were outside it.

(*Above*) Another fine prospect, this time from the Park at the bottom of Little Park Street. Cheylesmore Park once stretched from the city wall to Quinton Pool in Cheylesmore. In this open ground Coventry Races was ran from 1755 to 1783 becoming an important event in the County calendar. The Park, like much open ground around the city, was later taken in by various enclosure acts and was enclosed by hedge, fence and ditch.

(*Right*) A W. F. Taunton engraving dating 1869 of Bayley Lane. The lane takes its name from bailey of the motte (mound) and bailey (ditch) of Coventry Castle which stood on this site. Before 1300 it was spelt Bailley Lane, after 1400 it had changed to the present spelling of Bayley Lane. In the centre of the engraving is St. Mary's Hall one of the finest Guild Halls in the land. Next to it (right) is the only timbered building still standing in Bayley Lane. This building (c.1500) with its fine carved corner post was in 1869 the home of Mr. Brown the Baker; now it is simply number 22. Coincidentally behind this building once stood the castle bakehouse.

(*Below*) An 1860's impression of how the Pilgrims Rest in Palmer Lane looked in the 18th century. The Pilgrims Rest was in fact the guest house of the priory and provided accommodation for visiting pilgrims to the Cathedral who prayed to the many relics stored there. This building was almost entirely demolished in 1820 and replaced by a brick structure. When this second Pilgims Rest was being demolished in 1936, it was found to still contain parts of the original building consisting of timber, wattle and daub and stone tracery. This represented different stages of the earlier buildings suggesting that at its height the Pilgrims Rest was built of stone. During its earlier stage the narrowest section of the building in Ironmonger Row overlooked a large open triangular area where the towns market was held. This area was later infilled by the west side of Butcher Row; the east-side of Cross Cheaping; the south-side of Ironmonger Row and Little Butcher Row.

(*Above*) An 1860s engraving looking south up Great Butcher Row; across the top can be seen the 'Vaults' which led into Broadgate. Butcher Row was demolished to build Trinity Street in 1936-7 and the buildings on the left of the engraving stood where the flower bed now stands in Trinity Street. The earliest record of the street dates to 1309 when the city butchers were already established there. The lower section of the street which bordered the entrance to Coventry Priory was called the Bull Ring as it was here in 1424 that the butchers were ordered by the church to bait bulls before butchering. The left section below the sheep (running out of Priory Row) is the Bull Ring. H. Samuel now stands on the site including part of the site of the entrance gate to the priory precinct.

(*Left*) The Great Hall of St. Mary's Guild Hall, Bayley Lane engraved in 1869 and showing the scene set around 1825. Apart from new stained glass little has changed in the hall since that time or indeed the last four hundred years. The site of St. Mary's was granted by Guy de Tyllebroke (vicar of St. Michael's) to William Cole on condition that a lamp in his memory was kept burning on the high alter of the church. The guild to whom Cole belonged was the Merchant Guild of St. Mary and it was this guild which paid for the erection of the first hall in 1340.

The Hall used stonework and remains of existing buildings from the old Coventry Castle which were incorporated into the present building. These were part of the kitchen and Caesar's Tower (which was once four stories and embattled) and no doubt other now unrecognisable parts. The Hall was generally added to from 1393; this included the enlargement of the Great Hall to its present dimensions and the addition of the fine medieval truss roof decorated with fascinating carvings. The north window, as seen in the picture, replaced an earlier window in the late 15th century probably to coincide with the hanging of the magnificent and rather rare Arras Tapestry. The tapestry shows the marriage of Henry VII to Elizabeth of York who were members of the guildhall's main guild, the Trinity Guild. The border of the tapestry (now fairly faint) mixes white and red roses together signifying the union of the warring houses of York and Lancaster.

This Hall has had many famous visitors in the past including possibly Edward the Black Prince; definitely Henry VI, Henry VII, Mary Queen of Scots held prisoner here in Caesar's Tower in 1569. Princess Elizabeth, later the Queen of Bohemia (daughter of James I), was entertained here and presented with a gold gilt cup that was so large that it could not be held by the eight year old without the help of her soon to be guardian Sir John Harington of Coombe Abbey. In 1617 her father James I was entertained here followed by James II in 1687; his table was so full of food it collapsed under the sheer weight. Other notable visitors include Charles Dickens, George Eliot, Lord Tennyson and Sarah Siddons (England's greatest 18th century actress who played here).

(*Below*) The kitchen of St. Mary's as depicted by W.F. Taunton in 1869. The kitchen appears to be one of the earliest existing parts of the hall dating to around 1340-2. It is said that when Caesar's Tower was destroyed in the war, part of the exposed kitchen revealed itself as dating to the Norman period confirming that parts of the building were attached to Coventry Castle.

This area was buzzing with activity in the hall's heyday, especially when great feasts were held.

This is the beginning of a sequence of pencil drawings by Dr. Nathaniel Troughton who lived in Priory Row, Coventry. These are but a few of a much larger collection kept within the city archives and show scenes that would now be to most unrecognisable. Some of Troughton's scenes were based on older drawings but many just show street scenes which had simply remained unchanged for hundreds of years.

This first view shows Broadgate and Cross Cheaping on a busy market day in 1867. The last building on the left, butting out, is the Castle Hotel a popular 18th century inn. The scene on the right of the picture will be familiar to those who lived in the city before 1940. At the present this scene would be viewed by looking at Owen Owen from the steps of the National Westminster Bank. The use of Broadgate as a market place was a common theme throughout the city's history, this drawing however probably represents the last ever market held in Broadgate on December 2nd 1867. Vendors included market gardeners from Radford, fried fish sellers, confectioners, cheesemongers, crock sellers, bric-a-brac, and much more. From this last day, all that were allowed had to trade from the newly built Market Hall behind the Castle Hotel.

Troughton copied this illustration from an earlier drawing by John Eburne dated March 1822. It shows the demolition of ancient timber houses in Lower Broadgate and Cross Cheaping. The buildings opposite (the last on the right itself later demolished and replaced) represent the top of Cross Cheaping and next to the latter (off picture) stood the Vaults leading to Butcher Row. These buildings were felled as part of the process of widening Broadgate by the Road Improvement Act of 1812. The process began with Hertford Street and south Broadgate in 1820 and was nearing its completion in north Broadgate/Cross Cheaping in 1822. The reason for this destruction was to improve access for coaches and carriages; sounds familiar?

(c.1822)

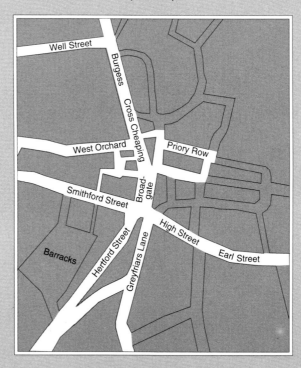

(*Left*) Troughton describes this as St. John's Bridges over the Sherbourne looking east. Drawn in the 1860's this scene is very eye-catching in its simplicity for their are still many who live in Coventry who are unaware we have a river. Both the Sherbourne and Radford Brook run under this spot we all now call the Burges. The Sherbourne can still be seen running underneath a building into the street from Palmer Lane; from here it is also notable that the buildings in the Burges are older than they appear and do in fact have Georgian faces. The Sherbourne was first believed to have been called the 'Cune' which is believed to be a Celtic or Early English name and some have suggested in the past that Coventry may have stemmed from this, i.e. 'the town on the Cune'; 'Cune-tre.' Sherbourne comes from the Saxon language and means 'Clear-stream,' and indeed trout could once be caught within the city precincts. Although by the later medieval period the river was often turned blue due to the work of the city's many dyers who specialised in the once famous

'Coventry True Blue.' The dye however being natural seems not to have totally destroyed the fish life in the river. The river itself is 10 miles long and rises near Corley Moor and ends joining the Sowe by Baginton.

The bridge in the drawing is probably medieval and is one of two shown on Speed's map of 1610. This particular bridge stood on the west side of the Burges where the present Argos shop now stands.

(*Centre*) A fine study of a courtyard off the east-side of Bishop Street as seen by Troughton. The entrance to the courtyard can be seen as a narrow passage on the right. In Troughton's time such courtyards were still

not uncommon in the city; a city which was considered one of the finest preserved medieval city's in Europe. These characteristic buildings were the everyday abode of the Coventrian, ancient oak-framed, infilled with daub and wattle or brick, or sometimes both. These building which probably dated to the 15th/16th century are but a reminder of what Coventry was and what it could have been.

(*Right*) In the foreground in Bishop Street stands Swines Cross named so because here was held the weekly pig market until its removal to the top of Bishop Street, then the Smithfield, in the late 19th century. The cross, which was probably medieval, was removed around 1763 and its base possibly used to support the font in Holy Trinity Church. Silver Street (background) dates from at least the 1290's and joined onto Cook Street leading to the gate. By its name we can assume at some early period it was a centre for silversmiths. The buildings on the right (slightly out of scale) backed onto the precincts of the Free School better known now to us as the Old Grammar School. The inn sign on the 16th century building is that of the Turks Head which was run by William King when Troughton drew this picture.

(*Left*) Looking down Bishop Street with the towers and spires of St. Michael's (left) and Holy Trinity (right) soaring, if not slightly exaggerated in the background. On the right is King Street, which mostly now lies under the Ring-road and left is Leicester Row, which suffered as the latter. The Castle Inn on the right is an 18th century building, but the older inn opposite off the picture was The Crane. This is the point on which Bishop Gate stood; a great square gateway controlling entrance to the city from the north. Some of these buildings did survive the war but nothing now remains.

(*Right*) Demolition work taking place in the middle of Palmer Lane (between present Trinity Street and the Burges) around 1860. The lane, which is probably the earliest track leading to Broadgate, got its name from the fact that pilgrims (Palmers) often walked up here to get to the priory or its guest-house which stood at the top of the lane at the junction of Ironmonger Row. In 1852 a large bunch of ancient keys, thought to have belonged to the priory, were dredged out of the Sherbourne in this lane together with numerous lead and pewter badges from various national shrines. Workman, such as those in the picture, unearthed here a 10in high statue of the Roman god Mars and later excavated a fragment from a saxon cross (it has recently been suggested that it may be a piece of door jamb), which was thought to have stood outside St. Osburgs circa 1016. The fragment is interesting for it bears a squirrel in a tree, not strong Christian symbolism but certainly symbolic of Saxon paganism. To the Saxon the squirrel in the tree represented 'Ratatosk' who darted up and down the 'Yggdrasil' the great Ash World Tree which joined heaven to earth. In the tree's upper most branches was an eagle thought to represent Odin/Woden and at its base the dragon 'Nidhogg.' Ratatosk darted between the two bearing spiteful messages, keeping them on their

toes. If this cross did indeed relate to Saxon pagan mythology it must be much older than realised and more probably have stood in the Saxon settlements centre

before the arrival of St. Osburg and her nuns around 700 A.D.

(*Left*) Looking up Fleet Street and Smithford Street around 1860. The drinking fountain on the left stands at the end of St. John's church. Behind it can be seen (as in many other drawings) a street gas lamp. The Coventry Gaslight Company built their coal gas works in Abbots Lane around 1820 and within four years many lamps had been erected in the city and the council were paying regular gas and repair bills. Behind the gas lamp can be seen Jackson's a provisions merchant. The building itself appears to be a large four storied Elizabethan building with a brick Georgian façade. The second building down from this marks the entrance to West Orchard, a road which passed the market and came out in Cross Cheaping. Beyond Smithford Street rises uphill towards St. Michael's. Note the man on horseback with large saddle packs slung across his horse he may have just left the building on the right, with the arch. This was an inn called The George the Fourth.

(*Right*) Looking east up West Orchard in 1865. This drawings main interest lies in the fact that it actually shows demolition underway for the new market hall which was opened on 2nd December 1867. In the background can be seen St. Michael's (right) and Holy Trinity (left). The buildings before them mark the bottom of Broadgate. The tall building in the centre stood next to the old pillared Market house in the Market Square (formerly the Peacock Yard) and was called the 'Watch-house.' Built in the early 18th century it was a police station cum place of short term detention in interior cells or the nearby stocks. West Orchard was first recorded by that name in the early 13th century and may have taken its name from an orchard associated with the early priory.

As Troughton states on this illustration, it is copied from another older drawing in the possession of a certain Mr. Burrows. The scene is set before 1793 when the inn was demolished for the building of the Coventry Barracks; home to Dragoons, Huzzars and later the Royal Field Artillery. The inn in question is the Bull Inn in Smithford Street which began life as the 15th century home of city Mayor Robert Onley. Here, after his coronation, Henry VII was entertained and presented with a gold cup and one hundred pounds. He returned the compliment by knighting Onley, making him Sir Robert. Henry stayed here again in 1487 while gathering an army which fought the Battle of Stoke; a result of this was that a pretender to the throne, Thomas Harrington, was brought to Coventry and Henry watched from this building as he was beheaded on the conduit opposite (the present site of Marks & Spencer). Another royal personage to grace the building, but this time as a prisoner was Mary Queen of Scots on the 25th November 1569. Mary was brought (by order of Elizabeth I) to the house, now the Black Bull Inn, by the Earls of Shrewsbury and Huntingdon. The latter however felt uneasy as there were Catholics in the area and informed the Queen. Elizabeth responded in anger and told the earls to remove the 'Scottyshe Queen' to more secure accommodation; this resulted in them moving her to St. Mary's Hall. Other stories connected with the inn involved the Gunpowder Plotters who stayed there in 1605 and, in 1642 as a Royalist army marched on the city led by Charles I, the City Recorder (Lord Northampton) tried to raise men to the royalist cause in the inn. The city was however for Parliament and Northampton had to flee for his life out of the inn's rear entrance at the Bull Yard. The inn was a much more extensive structure than the picture implies, as it had many extensions at the back and massive grounds stretching down to the present Bull Yard. This front section shows its medieval sandstone base and fine stone 15th century arch. The rest of the building appears to have been refaced in the late 17th/early 18th century.

(*Right*) Troughton describes this as number 18 High Street and numbers 1 & 2 Hay Lane. The 15th century buildings are being demolished in the year 1854 and were soon replaced with a brick built structure which for many years was a furnishers. The building is now more familiar as Yates Wine Bar opened in 1994. Note that number 2 has a door studded with iron nails; also note on number 1 the fine tracery in the upper window. Buildings such as these were once common in the city and favoured by merchants; the corner building has at some earlier period had its third floor overhang removed. It would have originally followed the lines of number 2. In the background can be seen the spire of Holy Trinity.

A wonderful view of Coventry from the Mill Dam, formerly St. Osburg's Pool and now Pool Meadow. The pool provided good fishing and was wooded nearly three-quarters of the way around. Amongst its many trees was one notable one called the 'Devils Ash' it was called so because it was believed that the devil was once seen in it. The ash stood near a small walled pool at the east end of this pool which was called 'Hobs Hole.' The hole was an ancient pre-Christian holy well which still at the time of this drawing had a pagan ceremony attached to it. On the left stands St. Michael, right Holy Trinity and next to Trinity the entrance tower of the priory ruins.

A Joseph Wingrave photograph showing the junctions of Smithford Street, Broadgate, High Street and Hertford Street in 1863. On the left is the City Hotel with its splendid wrought iron balcony. Across Smithford Street stands the King's Head which was one of the city's oldest coaching inns. The inn probably dated back to the 15th century and indeed cellars dating back to that period were discovered under the building when alterations were underway in the 1930's. Lord Nelson, and Lord and Lady Hamilton stayed here as did the Duke of Wellington.

Another, of less renown, who visited in 1822 wrote:

When last at Coventry I stopped to dine
At the King's Head, a house ne'er known to fail
In Worcester cyder and in Shropshire Ale.
The cutlet's came, rich and well done and smoking;
The host came too, a man much given to joking;
He brought a ponderous quarto [book], clasped and bound,
And read of old a wondrous tale. [Lady Godiva]

(*Right*) Another photograph taken by Joseph Wingrave around 1860. Wingrave was a chemist and druggist whose premises stood in the High Street (centre of picture). This photo, looking across Greyfriars Lane up the High Street, appears to have been taken from the small wrought iron balcony next to the Standard Printing Office. From the left stands Atkin & Son, tea and coffee merchants; this later became Atkins & Turton and Martins Bank. Its final use was as the Coventry Building Society before its demolition in 1990. Across Pepper Lane stands a fine 15th century building housing J. Tomkins, printer and stationer. This and the next building, dating from 1587, were destroyed in the November 1940 blitz.

(c.1860)

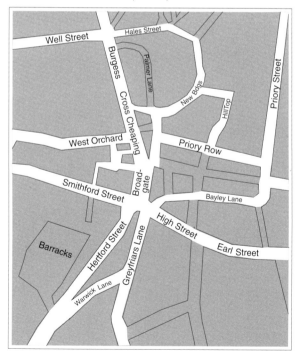

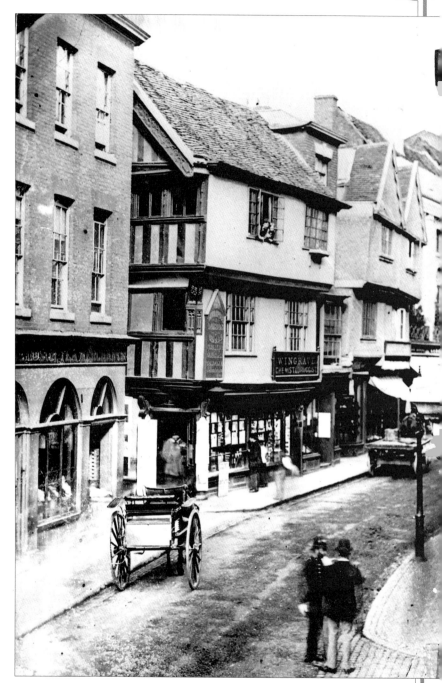

(*Left*) How Wingrave managed this view with a bulky plate camera is beyond me as it appears to be taken from the middle of the road at a height of about twenty feet. This extraordinary photograph (1860) looks down Smithford Street from the High Street. The cobbled area on the right is Broadgate; in the Coventry Times of 1870 is a sanitary officers description of this area. It goes thus: *Passing through Greyfriars-lane* [bottom left], *we soon reach the High Street, and thence emerge upon the market-place* [Broadgate]. *This open space which has a cab-stand in it, has been much modernised, and has the usual compliment of good shops and hotels, besides peeps of gabled High-street, and of a steep down-hill street sloping away from it. In contiguity to one side of the market-place, nestling under the shadow of the spire steeple of Trinity Church, and within a short distance of a well filled graveyard, are several plots of houses* [Butcher Row] *which are packed so closely together that the overhanging roofs make the light in the narrow streets subdued.*

Smithford Street, first recorded by its name around 1290, was steeped in history. At its lower end it crossed the Sherbourne via the Smiths-ford and later by the Rams Bridge. Examples of its history include prisoners who were held there during the Civil War in the Leather Hall (by the Lower Precinct ramp); the birth place of John Davenport, founder of the colony of New Haven, Connecticut; a pretender to the throne was beheaded on the site (occupied today by Marks & Spencer) in 1487; Mary Queen of Scots was held there in the Black Bull Inn until she was interred in St. Mary's Hall. This medieval inn (near entrance to Barracks Car Park) later became the site of Coventry Barracks in 1793 making Coventry a military city for over 100 years.

(*Right*) A Wingrave shot of Cross Cheaping and the Burges around 1860. Cross Cheaping was first recorded by that name in 1299 from the latin Forum Crucis which literally means the meeting place at the cross. This would imply that even at this early stage a market cross stood here. This may have some connection with the fragment of Saxon cross which was found nearby and can now be seen in the museum. The Burges as a name was recorded in 1309 and also before this period as Inter Pontes which literally means 'between bridges.'

This name is also reflected in Speed's map of 1610 when the street bears the name St. John's Bridges. The bridges referred to crossed the Sherbourne and Radford Brook at this point. St. John is taken from the nearby hospital and church of St. John of which the old Grammar School is a remnant.

Although this road is ancient, it is probably a re-routing of an earlier road which ran from behind the Grammar School to Palmer Lane. This track, which led to Broadgate and beyond, pre-dates the Roman period and at one point crossed the narrowest section of the great lake which lay in this valley. The crossing was a wooden causeway built on oak trunks sunk into the lake bed. Later, when the lake had all but disappeared, wooden fords crossed the river which remained until bridges were built.

Back in 1860, when this photo was taken, Coventry had a thriving population of 41,638. All however was not well as the weaving industry collapsed due to cheap imports and ribbons falling from fashion. The city's 25,000 weavers, and those in associated trades, were in dire straits; soup kitchens were opened and 4,000 emigrated.

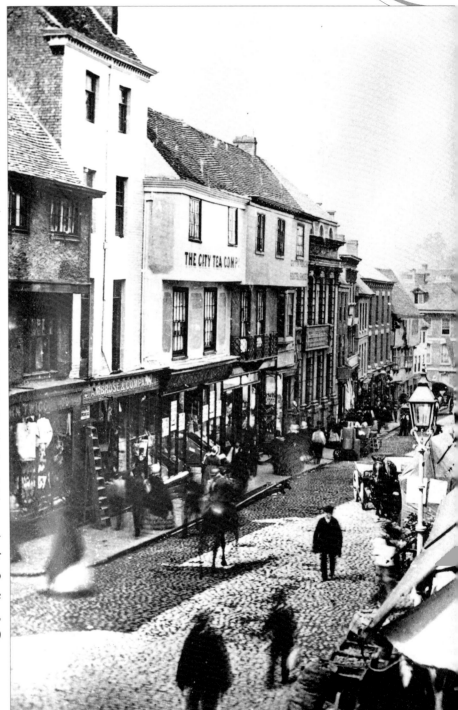

(*Right*) Looking north down Butcher Row in the 1860's. If you looked at this view today you would be standing near Cathedral Lanes looking at the flower bed in Trinity Street. Had this street survived, it would have been considered equal to the Shambles in York and as a conservation area it would have been lovingly tended and restored to its original beauty. Coventrians and tourists alike would have loved to tread these cobbles looking into period antique shops and little specialist companies. That is the dream of 'if,' the reality to our sanitary inspector in 1870 is as follows:-

Butcher-row and Little Butcher-row, may be particularly cited. In the heart of the city, close to the opulent market-place, under the shadow of two magnificent churches, and in the immediate neighbourhood of Priory-row, the butchers congregate (as they did in the middle ages), and slaughtering goes on in the public thoroughfare. As we past a sheep was slaughtered in this public way. A greasy bucket was held to receive the blood, which in time over-flowed and escaped down the steep gutter of the row. The houses once picturesque and clean, were pleasant residences when few people lived in each of them, and there was plenty of air from gardens in the rear, but converted into butcher's shops and offices, into slaughter houses and fish-mongers shops, by ugly cramped additions, and with living rooms excavated below them, they certainly form but a sorry substitute for a meat market.

(*Left*) An 1860's photo looking from Butcher Row and the Bull Ring down Little Butcher Row towards Cross Cheaping. This reflects many of Coventry's once well known late medieval back streets. The building on the right, with the gent at the door, was previously the home of a well know Coventry character called George Neale; so well known was he that on the 10th February 1849 the *Illustrated London News* reported his death.

We are reliably informed that, *He shuffled out of the world last summer, at Coventry, and was there buried with military honours, a few of the 11th Hussars and the 87th Regiment furnishing the firing party.* Neale was born in Coventry and spent part of his youth in the workhouse before being apprenticed to a japanner and then a butcher; before becoming a post-boy at the King's Head. At 18 he joined the navy and fought the French under Admiral Rodney on the flag ship 'Formidable'. His naval career came to a sudden end in 1782 when his leg was broken by round shot.

A few years later he signed up for the army serving Colonel Wellesley (later Duke of Wellington) amongst others in India. He was at the storming of Bagalore in 1791; the taking of Colombo in 1795 and finally the storming of Serinapatam in 1797. Here he received a fractured skull and numerous other wounds. After a fine naval and military career Neale was pensioned off in 1809.

During his military career we are informed that he received corporal punishment to the tune of '3000 to 4000 lashes.'

As an old man, Neale became a well known character who dressed in his military coats selling sage and thyme from his basket around the streets of Coventry. 'Georgie Neale,' as he was known locally, died at the age of ninety-three after attempting to walk back from Birmingham where he had been seeking his son.

A fine view of Broadgate and the top of Cross Cheaping around 1875. Hackney carriages line the centre of Broadgate either side of a portable waiting room which was wheeled out every day. The building behind the waiting room (Alexander) lay by the entrance to Butcher Row and Trinity Church. This was also the start of Cross Cheaping; it was by this point that the famed Coventry Cross stood.

about 15 minutes to refuel and get up more steam amid clouds of black smoke.'

It is not surprising that steam trams were not particularly popular and people reverted back to feet and horses. Things would however improve.

(*Right*) Children posing in Much Park Street outside Whitefriars Gate around 1875. This street, the name of which was first recorded in the 12th century, was originally one of Coventry's main roads leaving the city at New Gate onto the road to London. It once contained many fine stone-built houses of medieval Coventry merchants and notables such as Sir Henry Goodere.

In earlier times, Much Park Street led into the 'Great Park,' also known as Cheylesmore Park, which measured some 440 acres. Neighbouring Little Park Street (now the larger of the two) was a minor road which led to the 'Little Park' measuring 18 square acres. By the late 17th century both parks were united.

Whitefriars Gate as seen in the picture was an external gate to Whitefriars Friary which was surrounded by its own wall. It was built in 1352 and originally was much higher and had a solid oak door. The recesses above the arch once contained two stone figures connected to the friary — possibly the Virgin and St. Peter. It is believed Charles Dickens, who had passed this spot twice, refers to this gate in the Old Curiosity Shop, he wrote: *The moon was shining down upon the old gateway of the town, leaving the low archway very black and dark; and with a mingled sensation of Curiosity and fear, she (Little Nell) slowly approached the gate, and stood still to look up at it, wondering to see how dark, and grim, and old, and cold, it looked.*

There was an empty niche from which some old statue had fallen or been carried away hundreds of years ago, and she was thinking what strange people it must have looked down upon when it stood there, and how

(*Above*) This is one of Coventry's first steam-powered trams photographed soon after their introduction in 1884. The service operated privately by the Coventry and District Tramways Company ran between Coventry Station and Bedworth. The introduction of steam trams caused a sensation in the city when they first appeared, but many complained they were smelly, noisy and frightened the horses.

They were kept at the tramway depot on the Foleshill Road (near Lythalls Lane) and as the first tram left the depot one Coventrian recalled, "This was I suppose the greatest ever event seen in Foleshill up to that time. All Foleshillites were out lining the route as this 'iron horse' came jogging along blowing out smoke, for it was fed with coal like a locomotive.."

Another recalls the struggle of one tram getting up Bishop Street, 'Down Cross Cheaping it came, but it stopped at the bottom of Bishop Street to get up steam ready for the climb. All set and ready, chunk, chunk, chunk went the old engine, struggling up Bishop Street. When within about eight yards of the top it stopped, it refused to budge, so down to the bottom it came. It took

many hard struggles might have taken place, and how many murders might have been done, upon that silent spot, when there suddenly emerged from the black shade of the arch, a man............The street beyond was so narrow and the shadow of the houses on one side of the way so deep, that he seemed to have risen out of the earth.

(*Below*) A fine view of Greyfriars Green photographed around 1885. The green, which was originally

a public space and began to lay out the grounds as we see it here. The statute of a city benefactor, Sir Thomas White, was erected on the site of the old horse pool in 1882. The former pool, also known as the 'Red Sea,' was used by farmers and carters to tighten their wooden wheels and water their horses. Its nickname comes from the simple fact that when the clay, which lined the pool, was disturbed it turned the water red.

The horse pool had notorious origins for in the

common land on which freemen held rights to graze cattle, was also once known as Cheylesmore Green and 'Graffery Green' or Graffery (Greyfriars) Muckhill.' The name came from the fact that the Corporation up until the late 18th century used the green as a dumping place for the vast amounts of horse droppings which decorated the city streets.

The green was the home of Coventry Great Fair until 1858 when it was transferred to Pool Meadow and the green enclosed. The green ceased to be common land in 1875 and the corporation decided to turn it into

Coventry Leet Book under the date 1423 we are informed that there be a 'cokestowle [cuck-stool...ducking stool] made apon Chelsmore grene to punysche [punish] skolders and chidders as ye law wyll.'

Many of the houses on either side of the green still stand today; those on the right forming the 'Quadrant' were built on the old Sheriff's Orchard from 1870. Those on the left in Warwick Row began to appear as gentlemens residences from around 1764. These were built on the site of earlier buildings which were demolished for security during the Civil War.

(*Above*) A very fine view looking down Hales Street around 1890. Not one of Coventry's more ancient streets, it was built in 1838 to open up a congested section of the city. From left to right can be seen the end of the old Grammar School founded by John Hales from whom it is named. Behind the portable waiting room and hackney carriage, stands the Opera House newly opened in 1889, a building of varied entertainment such as opera, theatre, music hall and talks. Past the postered wall stands the entrance to Hinds & Co. Aerated Water Works suppliers of amongst other things fizzy lemonade in embossed glass bottles stopped with marbles. The long building still stands and was until recently Matterson's; the plough (removed 1995), was made by the company and placed on top of the building in 1880.

(*Right*) St. John's Church, Fleet Street around 1890. This church once affectionately called 'Johnny Boblick,' began life as a collegiate chapel founded by Queen Isabella in May 1344. Its purpose, amongst other things, was to receive prayer and take mass for the soul of her late husband Edward II and for her son Edward the Black Prince. Nearby Bablake College housed the priests who by the 1500's had reached 12 in number; plus 12 singing men. All was well until 1538 when, like many other religious houses in Coventry, the college and chapel were suppressed by the Crown.

From this time the building fell into disuse and was probably used as a store house. In April 1648 the building was used as a prison for Scottish Royalists taken at Preston during the Second Civil War. It is said that when these men were exercised in the city streets the people of Coventry shunned them, thus giving rise to the expression 'Sent to Coventry.' This however is only one of its possible origins, for Coventry was for hundreds of years a place of execution; individuals would be 'Sent to Coventry' and never spoken to again simply because it was a one way trip. These included Riband, the Priest who attempted to kill Henry III (1216-72) in his bedchamber at Woodstock. Riband was 'Sent to Coventry' to be 'torne by wild horses, and drawn thro' the streets til life leave bodie.'

After the Scottish prisoners had smashed the windows and generally defaced the interior, the city Recorder, Col. Purefoy, in 1651 gave his salary for the buildings to be repaired so that it could be used by the Independents. Later, the building was used as a market, winding house, even stables before finally becoming a parish church serving the Spon area in 1734.

As a building St. John's is most unusual in design and lay-out. It was built upon oak pillars driven into the old lake bed (sunk to a depth of 14ft 6ins) on which it stands. This lake reappeared in 1900 when the Sherbourne flooded and the interior was flooded to over five and a half feet. Despite its restoration in 1858-61 and 1875-77 by George Gilbert Scott, the exterior is now showing very bad corrosion from air born pollutants.

(*Right*) Looking down Little Butcher Row towards Cross Cheaping around 1890. This view has the odd quality of being a seaside town – one could easily imagine a fisherman sitting mending his nets. This however is part of the heart of old Coventry photographed from Great Butcher Row. Most of the buildings here date from the 15th to 16th century including those in the right-foreground which have later brick façades. The timbered building in the centre is rather extraordinary, because of its narrowness and height, standing three story's, plus an attic room. Interestingly, Little Butcher

Row in the 1300's was called Poultry Row because of the many poulterers. Also around here were potters, nearby Ironmonger Row was in fact originally called Potters Row. In 1936-9 John Bailey Shelton, the father of Coventry's archaeology to whom we all owe a great debt, excavated a number of pottery kilns around this area. Shelton said of one of these kilns, 'I believe the kiln was used for baking the vessels for use by the builders of the church [St. Mary's Priory Church] and closed on its completion.' He estimated the kiln dated from the 1300's at which time the priory was undergoing a major rebuild. No doubt after the hundreds of masons and other workers left after the completion of the job, the potters trade slackened and some time before 1410 the row became dominated by butchers and re-named Little Butcher Row.

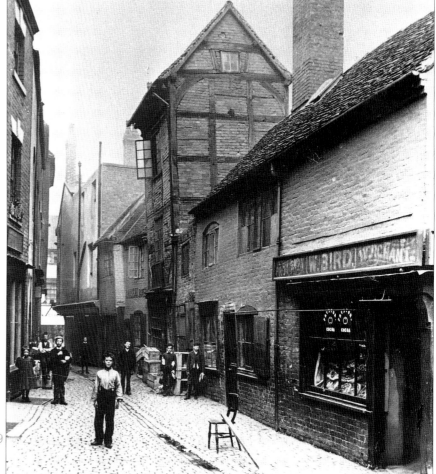

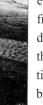

(*Left*) Looking up Hertford Street (left) and Warwick Lane (right) in 1898. On the far left stands the Peeping Tom Hotel with an image of Peeping Tom in the top window. This image now stands in the covered way in Hertford Street. Hertford Street itself was built in 1812-13 on land given by the Maquis of Hertford, who was Lord of Cheylesmore and also owner of Cheylesmore Park. Tradition states that the road was constructed after the Prince Regent complained when he passed here in 1807 about the difficulty negotiating the original main route, namely Warwick Lane and Greyfriars Lane.

In the foreground of the photograph, between Curtis and Beamish and the Temperance Hotel, stood until 1781 Greyfriars Gate, one of the city's finest gates built from stone from Cheylesmore Park granted to the city by Richard II.

Christchurch on the right was originally the church of the friary of the Greyfriars (Franciscans) who settled here around 1234 on land given by Ranulf, Earl of Chester.

(*Right*) A familiar sight to many Coventrians the old Free Library (later the Central Library) in 1898. The library was built partly on the site of Coventry Gaol which was demolished in 1871. The land was purchased by John Gulson (twice mayor of Coventry) and presented to the city. Gulson gave £2000 towards its building which was later supplemented by Samuel Carter who gave £1000. The new building opened in 1873 and contained over 35,000 lending volumes. The library had a reference section given once again by Gulson which was opened in 1890; this section contained 20,000 volumes. The section nearest to the camera was destroyed in the war but the rest survived and served the city well until its demolition for the building of Cathedral Lanes (opened 1990). If one looked at this scene in early 1871 one would see nothing but a 25 foot high brick wall following the lines of the library. Where the door is on the left marks the site of the city's last public execution; that of Mary Ball in 1849.

(*Above*) A fine view of Swanswell Pool in 1898. It began life as a much larger pool which filled the central valley of Coventry. However, during early times this large area of water silted up leaving the Swanswell and what became St. Osburg's Pool. Legend has it that the pool was formed by the rutting a giant boar which terrorised the area; the soil he threw up forming Primrose Hill. This giant beast was killed by the renown Sir Guy of Warwick (who is noted by some as being born in Coventry). The thigh bone of the animal hung for many centuries on Gosford Gate and became associated by many with the other fearsome beast he conquered, the Dun Cow. Sometime in the middle of the 19th century this bone for some unexplained reason was thrown into the Swanswell and has never been seen since. This legend, believe it or not, is thought to have given the pool its earliest name ...*The Swineswell*. The pool has been further reduced since this photograph was taken and more notably in 1851 when White Street was built. The pool has had a varied history, it has served

water mills since medieval times, and been used as a source of water when a pumping system was constructed in the 17th century. It has been a source of fish and a place of recreation for at one time a steam powered pleasure boat took passengers around the central island. In the background (centre) can be seen the first Coventry & Warwick Hospital built in 1864/5 and to the left of it Victorian St. Marks.

(*Below*) Idyllic Fords Hospital in 1898. Fords Hospital is one of the gems of Coventry and of the nation, firstly because it is considered one of the finest almshouses of its type and secondly it is largely constructed of teak – usually associated with coastal buildings. This wonderful time-machine (step inside and

"feel") was built on the site of probably the first Franciscan chapel. It was built in 1509 with money given by William Ford to house five aged men and one woman. In 1517 William Pisford further endowed the house extending its capacity to take in six elderly couples. Yet another William, William Wigston, left money in 1529 to house five more couples and pay them a weekly wage. By the late 18th century the house became exclusively female and so it is to this day. The quiet life of the Hospital was brought to a dramatic standstill on October 14th 1940 when it took a direct hit from a bomb. This resulted in the deaths of six inmates, a nurse and the warden; the building was shattered but still stood and in 1953 it re-opened after being lovingly restored using much original material from the rear of the building.

(*Above*) Young ladies in their straw boaters chat happily on the grass at the bottom of Greyfriars Green in 1898. The green is surrounded by fine wrought iron railings; these would disappear for munitions in the First World War. In the middle stands the statue of Sir Thomas White with the spires of the city pointing skyward; from left to right, Holy Trinity, St. Michael's and Christchurch. This particular section of the green has now disappeared.

(*Right*) People stroll around a not so busy Broadgate and Cross Cheaping on a sunny afternoon around 1899. Cabbies sit awaiting fares accompanied

by a fire-ladder which stood on this site for many years. This ladder appeared after the wife of Mr. Burdett, printer and stationer (building behind the ladder), died in a fire at the rear of the premises.

Two trams can be seen coming up Broadgate, one of which is on its way to the station. On the right of them can be seen a carriage with a fully livered driver waiting for its master or mistress to return from the nearby shops. Above the carriage stands a rare sight, a motor-car, probably a four horse-power Daimler. By the entrance to Butcher Row stands 'The Royal Wine & Spirits Vaults' belonging to Ind Coope & Co. and ran by W.F. Lane.

(*Below*) A particularly fine photograph taken in 1900 of Coventry's first electric trams on the Foleshill Road. Coventry's tram system was electrified in 1895 and the Coventry Electric Tramways Company ran trams from its Foleshill Depot from the 5th December 1895. The trams which ran between the depot and Coventry Station were initially looked on with some suspicion by those who feared the overhead power cables. However, the service soon proved a success as this Bank Holiday excursion photograph testifies. The system was expanded in 1897 to serve Bell Green and Stoke, 1905 Earlsdon and Chapelfields and as time passed many other parts of the city.

(*Right*) Tram number 20 passing through Broadgate to the Station. This handsome looking vehicle carried up to 52 people, not including the driver and conductor. Note on the upper deck the gents in the straw boaters. These are some of the Coventry Electric Tramway Company's

Beyond it are residential properties which would later be demolished for the new Hippodrome. All the buildings on the right appear to date from the mid-nineteenth century, built just after the street was created. The lower wall section, which is in fact brick pillars interspersed by wrought ironwork marks the site of the Smithfield. This was the city's cattle and livestock market opened by the City Council to bring the city's scattered livestock sales to one place.

So it was not unusual to see Hales Street blocked by cattle or sheep. The building at the end of the street is the Public Baths first opened July 8th 1852. These baths were extremely popular and, with an expanding population, were quickly outgrown. They were replaced by new baths in Priory Street in 1894 but the old baths stood for some years before being demolished for the fire station which opened in 1902.

management team. Also note that below the bench seats is a metal grill, this was often covered by a 'modesty board' to protect public decency and travelling ladies. In the background (left) is John Astley & Sons the oldest established company in the city which began life in 1730 as a high class seed merchant. Next door, and nearly as old, stands W & C Slingsby established in 1780 and brokers of Phoenix Fire Insurance and Pelican Life Assurance.

(*Right*) Looking east down Hales Street in 1900. On the left stands the familiar Mattersons building (now no longer occupied by the firm) and the familiar plough erected in 1880. The building at this point in time dealt mainly with agricultural implements, hence the plough.

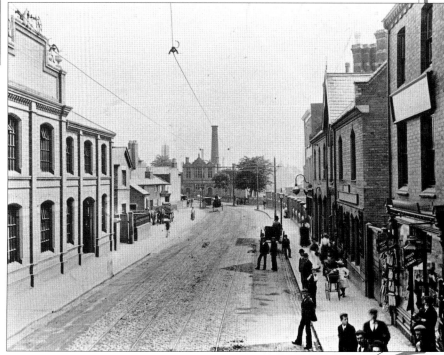

(*Left*) Looking up Hertford Street around 1900. The lady with the pram is just approaching the entrance to the Queens Hotel; in front of her can be seen the edge of the Post Office (still standing) and Johnson and Mason's purveyors of fine wines, spirits, beers, ales, ciders, champagnes etc. The building started life in the middle of the 19th century as the manufacturing warehouse of Messrs Wyley & Co, Chemical Manufacturers. It opened for trade as Johnson and Mason in 1885 and from its vast cellars (150 feet long) supplied the city and its surrounds, by waggon or from its off-licence. The building was demolished in 1929 to build the National Provincial Bank. The large building to the left of J&M's is the Corn Exchange, opened in June 1856 and built at the cost of £8000. The Exchange was used for concerts, talks, meetings and general purposes including the sale of corn. Its most famous guest was Charles Dickens who recited 'A Christmas Carol' here in December 1856. The Exchange later was converted and became the Empire Cinema.

(*Below*) Looking north down Little Park Street in 1902. Little Park Street (from the latin Vicus Parci Minori, leading to the Little Park) existed from at least the 13th century. The 15th century cottages, in the middle of the picture, were soon to be demolished and much of the street suffered badly some years later during the blitz. The Georgian building beyond (opposite the cart) still stands forlorn and boarded up as it has for some years. This building, from the 1730's, is stated in Penvenser's building bible to be one of the finest of its type in the country. The last building (opened June 1896) was until recently the Midland Bank on the corner of the High Street.

(*Right*) Looking west down Hales Street in 1905. On the right stands Mattersons and beyond the large building is the Opera House opened in 1889. This place of entertainment was very popular and provided opera, music hall, plays, recitals and talks by notables such as Sir Ernest Shackleton and Captain Webb of Channel fame. It was also the home for many years of the Coventry Repertory Company who took it through to the late fifties. Its last years were used mainly as a cinema and the building was finally demolished in 1961. The building behind it is the Old Grammar School and beyond that stands a shop on the corner of the Burges and Well Street. These shops were demolished for the building of Corporation Street opened in 1931.

(*Below*) Children stare at the photographer as he snaps Eaton Road in 1905. The number 22 tram heads of on its long journey back to Bedworth via the Foleshill Road after leaving its passengers at the entrance to Coventry Station. Eaton Road was opened in 1880 on land given by H.W. Eaton, Lord of Cheylesmore to serve Coventry Station which was opened in 1838. As well as watching the trains, the many young boys earned themselves the odd penny by helping people with their luggage when the porters were otherwise engaged.

(*Below*) A fine view of Fords Hospital in 1905. Note the extremely fine carving on the woodwork, something which makes the building so exceptional. Also note the timbered cottages below the Hospital; two fine possibly 15th century cottages now long gone. The building above them is also ancient by the visible timber-framing. The lamp on the left is actually attached to the Cheylesmore Inn formerly known as The Bell.

(*Right*) Few are unfamiliar with the legend of Lady Godiva; that she rode through the streets of Coventry naked to free the people from heavy taxes imposed by her husband, Earl Leofric. The legend was first chronicled by Roger of Wendover who was probably told the story around 1190 when evicted monks from Coventry came to his monastery in St. Albans. Roger gave two versions of the story, one saying the people stayed indoors and the other, the likely original tale, that the Countess Godiva rode naked through a full market place and was not seen by anyone; a miracle. Leofric thought so anyway and he himself was not adverse to the odd miracle for it is said he, together

called 'Brazen Face,' a sun and fertility god. Coventry revived the memory of Godiva in the 17th century when the Godiva Procession began and the story of Peeping Tom latched onto the legend. Over the centuries many women took the part of Godiva the earliest ones were usually actresses like Patsy Montagu in the photograph (1907) known by her stage name 'La Milo.'

(*Below*) Conductors, maintenance men and management pose for a Coventry Electric Tramways Company photograph taken at the Foleshill Depot around 1910. By 1912 the fleet of trams had grown to 42 open-top trams, mainly powered by Westinghouse engines. In the same year 11 new closed top trams were purchased bringing the total fleet to 53 vehicles.

with Edward the Confessor saw a miraculous vision of Christ. The reality behind the Godiva ride probably lies in the once common pre-Christian spring fertility ritual where a naked woman on horseback represented a goddess, possibly Epona. This was part of a procession which brought fertility back to the land and one such procession survived at Southam into the end of the last century. This had two Godiva's; one black and one white, led by a man in a bull mask

(*Left*) A pencil drawing of Palace Yard in Earl Street around 1910. The Palace Yard was one of Coventry's finest buildings and was built in various stages between the 15th and 17th centuries. It consisted of a double courtyard entered by a passage from Earl Street directly opposite the last bay of the present Council House. In the late 16th century it was the home of the wealthy Hopkins family. It was Sampson Hopkins who looked after the Princess Elizabeth here when she was threatened by the Gunpowder Plot in 1605. Another royal, James II, was entertained here in 1687 a year before he fled England. The king was wined and dined in what became known as the 'King James Room'; a beautiful oak panelled and decorated plaster banqueting room overlooking the main courtyard. The king was expected at Whitefriars but chose instead to stay at the 'Yard'

Palace Yard

because its then owner, Sir Richard Hopkins, was a Whig. The house left the Hopkins family in the 18th century and became an inn known as the Crown; it is said the large oak studded doors, which led into the yard, bore the inn's name and the coach arrival times. In the mid-19th century the inn became a builders yard, a ribbon warehouse etc, and generally fell into decay. This however was reversed in 1915 when craft-workers took over the building and gradually began a general restoration programme. By the time the craft workshop of Winifred King was opened to the public in 1927 the building was back to its former glory. All looked well for the future until the 14th November 1940 when the Palace Yard was completely flattened by a single high explosive bomb.

(*Below*) A fine summers afternoon at Nauls Mill pool and park in 1910. The pool began life as a mill pond fed by Radford Brook. It served a mill here from medieval times until 1889. The park was created at the turn of the century and the bandstand set up to provide weekend and evening entertainment, especially by local military bands. Music drifted across the park until 1953 and the bandstand was finally demolished in 1963.

(*Above*) The Lady Chapel, St. Michael's in 1912. At this time St. Michael's was the largest parish church in England and did not receive Cathedral status until 1918. The chapel, known as the 'Chapel on the Mount' due to its sheer height, once stood over the charnel house where excess bones from the churchyard were stored. In 1640 the church accounts show a charge of five shillings for 'cleansinge the charnel-house and laying the bones and skulls in order.' The chapel was also known as the Drapers Chapel because the Drapers Guild took responsibility for it and from 1518 when draper John Haddon, left money in his will to provide a priest 'to singe in the Chapell of our Ladye in the Church of Saint Mychell.' The drapers increased their obligation to the chapel in 1534 when it is recorded that 'Ev'y mastur shall pay toward ye makyng clene of oure Lady Chapell in saynt Mychell's churche and strawyng ye setus (seats) wt ruusches in somer and pease strawe in wyntur, everyone yerely 2d.' The chapel contained a number of interesting memorials including that of the Hon. Francis Wheler Hood, aged 32 (left of the window) of Styvechale Hall, a colonel in the Napoleonic War who fell in battle in 1814. His memorial shows him lying dead on the battle field with his regimental banner and cannons lying around. When it was taken down after the war to repair the wall, it was unfortunately damaged but instead of being repaired and returned it laid hidden inside the chapel for many years. The Lady Chapel stood next to the great east window and is now more recognisable as the site of Bishop Yeatman-Biggs'(died 1922) bronze tomb, which originally was placed in the centre of the chapel and is now under the window.

(*Below*) Greyfriars Green around 1912. Since our earlier visits to the green little has change except for the placement of the cannon surrounded by iron railings. This cannon was one of two siege pieces captured by Coventry lancers during the Crimean War. They arrived in the city in July 1858 and were first kept in Coventry Barracks. The guns both measured 8ft 2ins and were cast in 1799; both showed signs of being spiked and re-drilled; sometime after the turn of the century one gun was placed on Greyfriars Green and the other in Swanswell Park. This particular gun had its carriage badly damaged in 1940 as a straddle of bombs hit the green; in 1943 it was scrapped for the war effort.

(*Above*) Looking towards Spon Arches from Allesley Old Road in 1912. This area, along with Gosford Street, truly formed Coventry's late medieval suburbs; many of the cottages along the left although bearing brick façades date to the 15th/16th centuries. All these cottages are now gone and standing alone is the last of the row, the Black Horse inn, which dates to around 1800. The Black Horse has come under threat in recent years because of an unwanted scheme to widen the road. The visible arch, a section of Spon Arches, carries the Coventry to Nuneaton Railway Line. When the arches were first built they were the largest man-made structure in the area cutting through Spon End and straddling across fields. In 1857 the city was shocked to here that 27 of the arches had collapsed overnight; major rebuilding work finally got the trains running again.

(*Below*) Children sitting among the gorse on Styvechale Common in 1912. Behind them lies Earlsdon Avenue South and in the background, behind the trees, is the Kenilworth Road. This area was particularly beautiful with masses of mature oaks, rolling woodland and rough common; home to the now rarer grass snake and sand lizard. Children ran free catching newts in ponds, picking flowers and being one with nature, this was truly the Edwardian country idyll on the doorstep of Coventry. Note the handsome rustic fence curving to- wards the young women walking from the Kenilworth road.

(*Right*) The main entrance to the London Road Cemetery photographed in 1913. The memorial is dedicated to Sir Joseph Paxton who designed and personally supervised the laying out of the Cemetery in 1846-7. Sir Joseph was MP for Coventry from 1854 to 1865 and also once fulfilled the office as the city's mayor.

Paxton, who was once gardener for the Duke of Devonshire, has gone down in history as the designer of the Crystal Palace, erected in Hyde Park for the Great Exhibition of 1851 – considered one of the greatest feats of Victorian engineering. This memorial was erected after his death in 1865 and was familiar to the many Victorians who promenaded these grounds on Sunday afternoons; a practice which seems was still in vogue in 1913.

(*Right*) Looking down Bayley Lane in 1913. A view little changed by time and perhaps the finest view in the city. Time passes by, peoples clothes change but Bayley Lane remains. The lane is thought to follow the line of the castle ditch (bailey) which I believe ran within the site of St. Michael's. The earliest section of St. Michael's, when it was a chapel, stood on this left section in the photograph, this would have probably stood just within the Bailey of the castle.

The Starley Memorial in Queen's Grove, off Queen Victoria Road in 1913. James Starley the 'Father of the Cycle' was from childhood an inventive genius. He was born the son of a Sussex farmer and finding farming dull left to seek his fortune in London. He never reached the capital but spent 15 happy years working for the Wilson Family in Lewisham. James married and had three children before finally moving to London and finding employment with Newton, Wilson & Co. During this time he invented a new type of sewing machine and met Josiah Turner who talked him into setting up their own business in Coventry – a city full of skilled labour but mass unemployment due to the collapse of the weaving and watch making industries. James Starley arrived in Coventry in the summer of 1861 and with Turner and others set up the Coventry Sewing Machine Company in King Street. Turner's nephew became the company's agent in Paris and got wind of the new 'boneshakers' which had become fashionable.

During November 1868 he arrived back in Coventry and caused quite a stir as he rode a boneshaker from the Station to the King Street factory. Starley and Turner viewed the new machine with interest and decided this is where the future lay; renaming the company the Coventry Machinist Company they went into the production of cycles. Not satisfied with the foreign cycle, Starley looked at ways of improving it and with the help of William Hillman patented the 'Ariel', the first light weight all metal cycle with tension wheels and tightenable spokes. From his home at 18 Upper Well Street Starley often beavered in his workshop inventing new things such as the differential gear, cycle speed gears, and 15 other revolutionary patents. In June 1881 he attended Queen Victoria at her request and gave her two of his 'Salvo' tricycles, these thereafter became the 'Royal Salvo.' In that same summer he was diagnosed as suffering from terminal cancer, despite this he worked on at King Street and at home in Well Street. In his home workshop Starley worked on a highly advanced sewing machine but, racked with pain and frustrated by delays, smashed it to pieces. Within the month he was dead. James Starley was 51 when he died and many believed Coventry owed him a great debt as he had pointed the way to the city's future. A public subscription raised £335 to erect a memorial and this was unveiled before a crowd of eight thousand people to the strains of 'The Conquering Hero.' Starley's widow later lived in Starley Road until she died. The Starley family continued making their mark on the city with Starley Cycle's and John Kemp Starley, James' nephew, invented the first safety cycle from which all modern cycles and the Rover Motor Company were derived. The Starley Memorial was moved to the end of Warwick Row when the Ring-road was constructed. The figure on top of the memorial represents fame leaning on the anchor; a symbol of hope for Coventry's future.

A busy Broadgate and Cross Cheaping in 1914 just before the outbreak of war. Little did the people of Coventry know what lay in store; many Coventrians joined their local regiment the Royal Warwicks and fought on the bloody battle fields of Europe. Thousands of young men left the city; 2,587 never came back. Of the villages that surrounded the city all paid the price in the 'war to end all wars.' Note the tram on the left, under its number can be seen an X. This denotes that the number 9 tram runs from Broadgate to the Allesley Road. This new system was for the benefit of those citizens of the city who were illiterate. Note also that the tram on the right carries the logo 'Hansons Pianos.' This company traded from number 20 Hertford Street selling a wide range of musical instruments.

(*Left*) Looking up Hertford Street from Warwick Road in the summer of 1914. A typical sign of summer is the wearing of straw boaters, replacing the Coventry flat cap. The large building is the Rover Company's office and showrooms which fronted the company's earliest workshops. Next door stands the 'The Tunns Commercial Hotel', an original coaching inn standing from at least 1750. Above the old coach entrance can now be seen the word 'Garage' indicating the advancement of road transport. Across the entrance to the Bull Yard stands the Peeping Inn (later Hotel) which was originally the Railway Hotel.

(*Left*) A fine view of St. Michael's from Pepper Lane around 1919. On the left is the junction to the now gone Derby Lane which earlier bordered the rear wall of Coventry Gaol. Connected to the gaol, which closed in July 1860, is the prison governor's house which is attached to the 18th century court house. A prison stood on this site from at least the 17th century; in its final stage it had a numbers of wings for male and female prisoners, a chapel, court yards for exercise and a treadmill. It was on a morning such as this in 1846 that Mary Ball, the last to be executed in the city, was hung on a black-draped scaffold before a crowd of thousands of people as the bell of St. Michael's struck eleven.

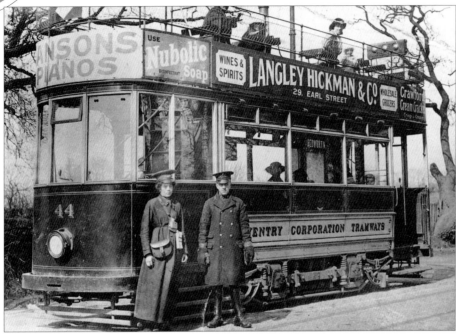

(*Left*) The number 44 halts in open countryside on its journey from Coventry Station to Bedworth. Note that the tram now carries the name of the Coventry Corporation Tramways – the tramway system was purchased by the City Corporation in 1912 from the Coventry Electric Tramways Company for £202,132. The actual length of track in use at this time measured 13 miles. This particular photograph was probably taken around 1915 when women conductors first appeared replacing the men who had gone to war.

(*Right*) Cook Street Gate from Cook Street in 1914. The gate, one of the city wall's minor gates, was erected in the 14th century and is one of only two remaining in the city (the other being Swanswell Gate). The doorways into this gate can still be seen about 20 foot off the ground. These led into guard-rooms in the upper section of the structure. This gate led to the Leicester road and outside it are buried three suicide victims, including one called Johnstone who in 1619 poisoned eight inmates of Bonds Hospital before poisoning himself. In front of a huge crowd, Johnstone was buried at midnight on the roadside outside this gate. By the late 19th century Cook Street Gate had become derelict and it was eventually presented to the city by Sir William Wyley in 1913 to be restored in 1918 and 1931. On the left stands the Old Tower Inn (earlier the Old Tower Tavern) which was built in the 16th century and presented to the city by the brewery as a building of historic interest. Despite this it was demolished in 1963.

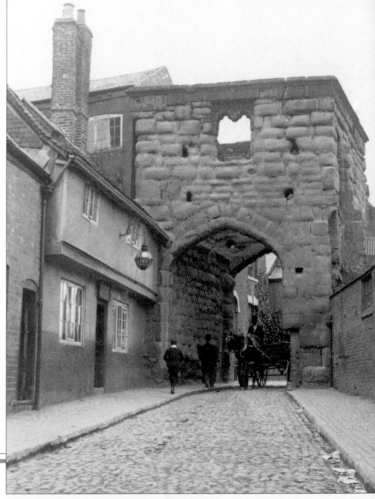

(*Left*) A unusual view of Bonds Hospital from the garden around 1917. Three inmates stand chatting and looking at the tulips. This garden would have originally been much smaller because up until 1662 the city wall ran through here from Hill Street Gate towards the left of the picture. These almshouses were founded by Thomas Bond, a Coventry draper who in 1510 left money for the erection of a hospital to accommodate 10 aged men. The building was enlarged in 1816 and restored in 1832-4 and 1846-7. During the latter restoration the Elizabethan style chimneys were added; these however were blown off in the blitz. The hospital, now further extended, still serves its original function. Beyond the building on the right lies the quadrangle which is shared with the old Bablake School (founded 1560).

(*Right*) Looking down Broadgate and Cross Cheaping in 1917. Cabs ply for fares as a tram rattles up the hill; a motorcar trundles downhill past a horse-drawn gig. A man relieves his thirst from the water fountain to the left of the fire ladder. Note, on the left, the shop of W.H. Icke who advertises himself as a Furnishing Ironmonger who amongst other things sells guns, rifles and Kynoch Cartridges. Next door stands the once better known Maypole which began life as purveyors of dairy products and ended as supermarkets.

(*Left*) St. Michael's photographed in the year of its upgrading to cathedral status in 1918. The church was built mainly between the 14th and 15th centuries on the site of a chapel which stood here from at least 1138. In reality the church stands on the summit of a hill which is probably why it was dedicated to St. Michael who, for some unknown reason, is connected with hill tops. The tower was finished in 1394 and paid for by local merchants William and Adam Botoner. The spire, begun in 1432, was paid for by their sisters Mary and Anne who, it is also claimed, also paid for the church and choir. The completed tower and spire, heavily decorated in perpendicular style, is considered one of the finest in the land and the third tallest (was 300ft, now about 294ft). Sir Christopher Wren, when a resident at Wroxhall, visited Coventry and declared the church to be an architectural masterpiece.

(*Right*) Members of the Warwick Lane Wesleyan Chapel Sunday School photographed behind the old Methodist Hall dressed to take part in the Godiva 'Peace' Procession on July 19th 1919. The gentleman on the right, wearing a hat, is John Bailey Shelton who came to Coventry from Nottinghamshire in 1897. John was from a farming community but came to the city as he had Wesleyan friends here. He attended the Wesleyan Chapel (now Central Methodist Hall) and soon met and married another Wesleyan, Catherine Aston. John was determined to start off his own haulage business which became established in Little Park Street. His great love for animals shone through as he soon found himself running a shelter for stay animals. In addition, John spent much time working with the children at the Wesleyan Chapel and befriending the inmates of the Workhouse

and Hospital in Gulson Road. In 1923 he became involved in civic affairs becoming a member of the Board of Guardians. However, John is mostly remembered for his work spent saving Coventry's past for which he earned the nickname 'Father of Coventry's Archeology.' Wherever there was a hole in the ground 'JB' would be there if he hadn't dug it himself he would be checking it. It was through such work that he set up his own 'Benedictine Museum' in Little Park Street.

John was appointed City Chamberlain in 1945 and in 1956 was awarded an MBE for his dedication to the people and history of Coventry. 'JB' presented his great collection of Coventry's past to the new Herbert Museum in 1957 forming the core of its collection. His life abruptly ended in November 1958 when he was struck by a motor cycle. A week later aged 83 John Bailey Shelton died leaving behind him many sad people but one great legacy to the city.

(*Below*) The Godiva 'Peace' Procession wends its way through Broadgate on Saturday July 17th 1919. The procession officially celebrated the end of the war with nearly 20,000 school children gathered in Pool Meadow. A celebration in prayers was held at St. Michael's and at 3.00 p.m. Gladys Mann, daughter of Councillor Cleverley, played Lady Godiva and led the parade through the streets of Coventry. On this occasion, and for the first time, Godiva appeared fully clothed

abruptly to an end by rain. Soon after, and for no apparent reason, crowds began to gather in Broadgate and after much shouting the King's Head Hotel came under attack from a mob armed with bricks and stones. The police quickly arrived and then the mob turned on them showering them with bottles and bricks. The police regained control and the rioters went home. The following evening it began anew and more shops in Broadgate were attacked before the police again took control of the situation. It was noted that

women were supplying the rioters with broken bricks gathered in their aprons from a building site in Market Square. Rioting began again the following night but this time with looting. The police, assisted by office staff, were issued with batons and fought running battles with the mob driving them down Cross Cheaping and dispersing them into

in a beautiful and intricately detailed Saxon dress. The procession was a great success, ending with children waving flags and a display of fireworks.

(*Centre*) This is Broadgate on the morning after the Godiva 'Peace' Procession. The previous evening was coming to a happy conclusion, although brought

the side streets. This was the last act of rioting and for three days the citizens of Coventry were put under curfew. Some say the riots began as rumours were spread that certain shops in Broadgate were German owned, this however was not an isolated case for 1919 saw many riots throughout England as soldiers were demobbed and found themselves unemployed.

(*Right*) Peeping Tom looking down on Hertford Street from the top storey window of the King's Head Hotel in 1920. The figure of Peeping Tom is generally believed to have been added to the story of Lady Godiva in the mid-17th century. Legend from that time states that Tom was the only one to look at the noble lady and for his voyeurism was struck blind. This story can be found in classical texts referring to even more ancient 'peeping toms.' Recent evidence however suggests that the story may have originated with the Corporation's commission of a Godiva painting in 1586. When this painting was cleaned in 1976 a bearded figure came to light looking out of an upper storey window. People may have later considered this to be Peeping Tom when in reality it was probably meant to represent Earl Leofric. The actual image of Tom is generally agreed to be a 15th century oak sculpture of St George who legend declared was born and died in Coventry. He was born to Lord Albert at Caludon Castle; stolen and brought to manhood by Kalyb the witch, became the seventh Champion of Christendom and brought the other six champions to Coventry before setting off questing on foreign shores. Local legend states St. George returned to Coventry with a princess and lived his life out here in peace. A second legend claims that George came back to save the people of Coventry from a great dragon which came from a cavern under present day, Hill Top. A great battle ensued and finally the beast was slain; as for St. George he died from his wounds and was buried in state in Coventry. Processions in his honour were led every year around the city which were later taken over by Lady Godiva but a figure representing George always still appeared before the Lady. The oak figure of George, which originally probably straddled a dragon, is thought to have come from either St. George's Chapel, which stood in Gosford Street, or more likely from the lost Priory of St. Mary because amongst its list of relics is included, 'an image of St. George, with a bone of his shielded in silver.' In 1659 the figure had its arms cut off so it could be placed at a window by Coventry Cross at the junction of Broadgate and Cross Cheaping. In 1678 Alderman Owen had the figure placed in a window at his house at the bottom of Greyfriars Lane. When that house was demolished around 1775 city antiquarian and hatter Thomas Sharp obtained the figure and placed it in a specially constructed nook in his shop near the top of Smithford Street. When Hertford Street was constructed in 1812-13 Sharp's shop became the corner building and Tom acquired a new nook looking towards Broadgate and down Hertford Street. In the 1870's the King's Head was rebuilt on a larger scale taking in the corner of Smithford and Hertford Streets; Tom soon found a place in the hotel looking out from his own forth storey nook (as seen in the photograph). Tom stayed here until 1934 when he was taken into the hotel. It was the intention of the management to replace the original with a head and shoulder copy while the original was restored and

protected from the elements. The plan however never materialised and in 1940 the hotel was destroyed. Tom later appeared in the Hotel Leofric and now stands in a glass case overlooking the statue of Lady Godiva from Cathedral Lanes.

(*Below*) Numbers 122 to 125 Much Park Street around 1920. The buildings on the left half of the photograph belonged to the Midland Brewery which supplied the local area using huge horse drawn carts lined with barrels. The building, which dates from the

mid-15th century at the back and the 16th century at the front, was once known as the Green Dragon Inn. This was the inn referred to by George Eliot in her book 'Middlemarch' which was based on her memories of Coventry. The building was taken down in 1982 and re-erected in Spon Street. Number 124 however, with the fine gabled section bearing the sign, did not survive. Before they were removed, much of these buildings were used by H. E. Hamerton & Sons, Ribbon dyers and finishers. Note on the beam between the long window and first boxed window is a lead fire Insurance mark of the Sun Fire Insurance Company. This meant that should the building catch fire it would be dealt with by a fire engine manned by employees of that particular company.

(*Left*) Looking north down Great Butcher Row in 1920. Frank's the Furnishers take up a fair section of cobbles displaying their wares in the street. If we compared this view to today, all the buildings down to the horse and cart are now the flower bed in Trinity Street. Below is the Bullring running from the corner of Priory Row. On the left is A.W. Garlick, hardware dealer; to the right of it, the building with the apex facing the street (near the bottom) is the Spotted Dog pub which was built on the site of the entrance gate to the Priory.

(*Below*) Looking towards the great east window of St. Michael's around 1920. The east window was divided into five sections with the central three sections containing glass dedicated to the memory of Queen Adelaide and dated 1853. The two figures of St. Peter and St. Paul were placed in the piers in 1861. The pulpit (right) was very unusual for it was made in 1869 of brass and wrought iron; the work of Coventrian Frank Skidmore. Skidmore was considered one of the greatest metal art workers in the land and his work still stands on the Albert Memorial in London. Prince Albert was also commemorated in the old cathedral by a window in the Lady Chapel – visible through the piers on the left.

(*Left*) Greyfriars Lane and Fords Hospital in 1920. This photograph really shows the narrowness of the lane which, before 1813, was the main road into the city from the south-west. This narrow lane has seen monarchs, armies, and time pass by. It is indeed an ancient road going back before written history taking the traveller south towards Baginton. One person who passed here more recently was George Eliot; it is said that she used to cut through Fords Hospital and the rear garden to get to Cow Lane Chapel where the Rev. Francis Franklin used to preach. Franklin was the father of her much admired teachers at Warwick Row School, he like many others she knew appeared as a character in one of her novels. Note the fine cobbles in the lane which also form the pavement. The house on the right is very rarely seen on old photographs and appears to date from around 1700. The sandstone foundation may however imply it is a refaced older building.

time the priory fell. The pulpit dates to about 1470 and is one of the tallest in England and also considered stylistically the most important. For many years the perpendicular pulpit had been encased in wooden panelling with a seat for the verger at its base. It was however re-discovered when the building was being restored in 1833. The brass lectern dates from the 15th century and during the Commonwealth was used as a collection box with money placed into the birds mouth. Beyond can be seen fine 15th century choir stalls many of which carry fine carvings (mesicords) under their seat. One, a particularly fine example of a Green Man, is a pre-Christian nature god who was adopted by the British church. Two of the same ancient images can be found at either end of the Marler's Chapel. The Victorian east window was destroyed in the blitz and replaced with the present 'Brides Window.' George Eliot and her father attended Trinity.

(*Right*) Looking down the chancel and south aisles of Holy Trinity Church in 1921. Holy Trinity began at an uncertain date as a chapel connected to the Priory Church of St. Mary. This early church was already old in 1391 for its chancel was described as being 'ruinated and decayed' and its rebuilding was paid for by the Priory of Coventry. The present building dates between the early 13th and late 15th century. Within the pre-Reformation church was the main alter dedicated to the Trinity and numerous chapels tended by priests; numbering one vicar, eleven parochial priests and two chantry priests. This all came to an end at the same

(*Left*) A family snap taken outside Cook Street Gate around 1925. The building on the right was probably erected in the late 1830's after the wall on the site was cleared. Through the arch can be seen the Old Tower Inn and cottages beyond. On the gate itself can be seen signs of its restoration in 1918 and there is little to show that this gate once bore a portcullis and drawbridge which gave access across the long gone moat. Cook Street Gate was always a favourite on old postcards where it was sometimes referred to as the 'Old Tower' or even 'Broadgate' by postcard producers who lacked local knowledge.

(*Below*) This 1925 view has hardly changed. We see inmates of Bonds Hospital (left) in the quadrangle formed with Bablake School (right). The building was founded in 1506 by the will of Thomas Bond, former mayor and draper, to house ten aged men and one aged

woman; the woman however was a housekeeper and not an inmate. The inmates, who had to dress in black, were in perpetual mourning for their benefactor and had to attend nearby St. John's on a daily basis as part of their contract. Apart from enlarged lower windows this part of the building seems to have changed little externally since its foundation, especially since the later chimney pots were blown off in the blitz. Bablake School was originally part of the College of priests attached to St. John's. The building built in the 15th/16th centuries was used from 1560 as a 'hospital' for boys who were educated here and then placed into apprenticeships. In 1890 the school had outgrown the premises and a new Bablake was built on the Coundon Road. There is a peculiar story attached to Bablake's foundation in that Thomas Wheatley, a wealthy merchant, had ordered a chest of iron ingots from Spain. The chest came back to him, not full of iron ingots but silver ingots. As Wheatley had already paid for his 'iron' he did not pursue the mistake and it is said that with some of his new found wealth founded the 'Hospital' which later became Bablake School.

(*Below left*) What follows is part of a series of postcards produced and sold in the 1920s and early 1930s. The illustrations were the work of Florence Weston, once a very popular and still sought after Coventry artist. Florence, although producing these pen and ink drawings was known more for her lovely watercolours and oil paintings. The first is 'Old Gabled Houses in Butcher Row.' This particular drawing is somewhat confusing because Florence chose to curve Butcher Row to emphasize the gabled buildings. These buildings were in fact at the top of Butcher Row on the south-east side, and the two with the finely carved gables were the shop of Frank's Furnishers.

A very busy rush hour junction of Broadgate and High Street around 1924. Note the original narrowness of the High Street. On the right stands the National Provincial Bank and the Coventry Arms, both were demolished in 1929 for the building of the present National Westminster Bank (then National Provincial). The Coventry Arms (with the white pillars) had a 14th century cellar and much of the building was 16th/17th century. Like many ancient Coventry buildings its age was hidden by a modern façade. Further down the street can be seen a 16th century merchants house, this was demolished when the street was widened in the '30s.

(*Right*) 'Coventry. St. Mary's Hall & Old Curio Shop looking West.' The name plate on the door of the timbered building (c.1500) reads 'Owen'. This drawing, like others in the series, reflect an earlier period. Number 22 Bayley Lane was a bakers in the last century then later a curio shop.

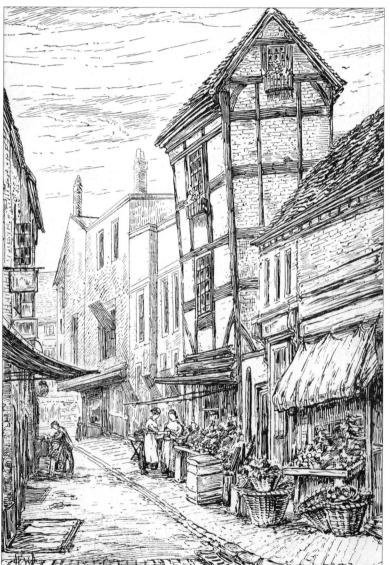

(*Above*) Butcher Row, Coventry. This view looks south from the entrance to Priory Row. On the right, the timbered building with items displayed outside, is Garlicks Ironmongers and further down can be seen the barbers pole prominently displayed outside the barbers shop. The building, corner left, has had its ground-floor converted into either a store room or garage. When these buildings were demolished the corner property was found to stand on a fine 15th century vaulted cellar, which like many others, was unfortunately filled in.

(*Right*) Looking west down Little Butcher Row towards Cross Cheaping. On the right the corner shop appears to be selling mainly vegetables, as does the tall building which was earlier known as the 'Olde Curiosity Shoppe.'

impossible to say exactly what they originally were. The window next to the door looks into the Mercer's Chapel. Above is the Venetian window of the Mayoress' Parlour, a room along with that in Caesar's Tower with which Mary Queen of Scots was associated. The half-timbered section on the right forms the entrance to the hall and above is the Drapers Room, used for guild meetings. The iron door on the left leads into the crypt and next to it stands a stone known as 'Lady Godiva's Mounting Block' – a horse mounting block used by various Godiva's from the 17th century. The window above runs along the east wall of the Great Hall and contains stained glass depicting royalty associated with the city.

(*Right*) This drawing has the extended title,' St. Mary's Hall. Coventry. Crypt Door, Lady Godiva's Mounting Block & Carved Gateway in Courtyard.' The entrance porch at the north end of the courtyard probably belongs to the original hall built in the 1340's. The carvings either side of the entrance have for many years been worn smooth by the elements and it is now

(*Below left*) Entitled 'Whipping Post & Figure from Ancient Cross. Old Kitchen, St. Mary's Hall. Coventry.' The Knave's Post was originally a post to which criminals were tied and whipped. Later it was set into a building in Much Park Street and villains were tied to carts and whipped from the post to the Mayor's Parlour in Broadgate and back. The figure was placed in the kitchen in 1900 and is now in the museum. The figure from 'the ancient cross' is that of Henry VI which graced Coventry Cross (completed 1543) until it was demolished in 1771. Note the corbels including the angel holding the shield which bears the letters I.B. The arches on the left originally led into another section of the building; they appear to have been blocked off at an earlier date.

(*Below right*) Members of the management of Coventry Corporation Tramways take delivery of two new buses outside the Council House (built 1913-17) in 1925. The gentleman (second from left with hat and moustache) is Thomas Whitehead the Corporation Tramways manager who came to Coventry in 1895 to organise the new electric tram system. He did this and also introduced the omnibus before the First World War. Whitehead believed the bus was the future and extended the bus service throughout the city. The bus on the right is a 52 seater Maudsley which was exhibited at the Commercial Motor Show in London and acquired by the Corporation. Both these buses have solid tyres; pneumatic tyres were not used until 1927.

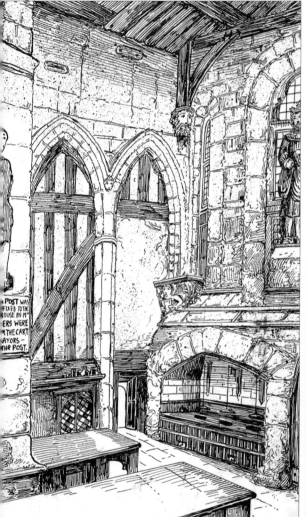

Looking down Priory Row in 1926. Priory Row probably originally led to the Bishop Palace, residence of some of the medieval bishops of Coventry. The lane was realigned to its present straightness in 1807. On the right stands the entrance to Blue Coat School built in 1856. The timbered building is still recognisable today and was once called Lych Gate House because a lynch gate stood near the entrance to Priory Row. The building was built on the remains of one of the old priory entrance towers by the Rev. John Bryan, vicar of Holy Trinity around the year 1648. The building beyond this point leading to Butcher Row were demolished in 1936.

(*Left*) The Kenilworth Road, 'Long Avenue' around 1925. This view, taken from Gibbet Hill, shows what must be one of the most handsome roads in England. The road is three miles long and joins Coventry to Kenilworth and runs across land originally belonging to Stoneleigh estate. As the photograph shows, the road was a popular venue for cyclists, it also was regularly used by early motorcar manufacturers as a test track. On the right was the spot where Baker, Drury and Leslie were hung and gibbeted in 1765 for the murder of Stoneleigh farmer Thomas Edwards. Their bodies hung here for years and the gibbet stood for over 40 years giving Gibbet Hill its name.

(*Above*) Looking down Cross Cheaping in 1925. Here we see how the road sweeps down to the Burges and up Bishop Street. The tram-post and inspectors hut mark the boundary of Cross Cheaping and Broadgate.

to provide a fine vista when entering the city from this direction. The houses on the left were known as Landsdowne Place and one of the buildings bears the logo LNWR of the London North Western Railways. The back of the sign in the foreground is that of Perkins & Son, Nurserymen who were situated next to the Railway Goods Yard. In the distance can be seen the two domes of the United Reform Church in Warwick Row and beyond the Clock Tower of Coventry Market Hall. On the road in this wonderful photograph can be seen various forms of transport including a gig, motorcar, motor bikes and sidecars, horse-drawn flat waggons, horse-drawn covered waggon, a lorry and even a handcart.

(*Above*) Thomas Whitehead the manager of the Coventry Corporation Tramways proudly sits (far left) with the Mayor and others for a publicity photograph for a special tram decorated and illuminated to raise funds for the new war memorial. The war memorial was unveiled in the Memorial Park on 8th October 1927 by Field Marshal Earl Haig . The park was opened in 1921 on 121 acres of land acquired from the Gregory-Hood's of Styvechale Hall. Similar trams to this ran on certain occasions such as special anniversaries or Christmas.

(*Right*) Looking down Warwick Road towards Greyfriars Green in 1928. From the left can be seen Queen Victoria Road and to the right the junction of Eaton Road and St. Patrick's Road. Warwick Road was widened after the opening of Coventry Station in 1838

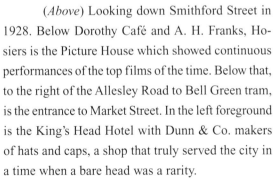

(*Above*) Looking down Smithford Street in 1928. Below Dorothy Café and A. H. Franks, Hosiers is the Picture House which showed continuous performances of the top films of the time. Below that, to the right of the Allesley Road to Bell Green tram, is the entrance to Market Street. In the left foreground is the King's Head Hotel with Dunn & Co. makers of hats and caps, a shop that truly served the city in a time when a bare head was a rarity.

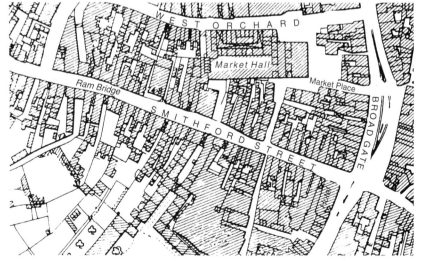

(*Left*) Looking down Smithford Street from the junction with Broadgate in 1929. On the left stands the Kings head Hotel and on the right the Dorothy Café standing above the Picture House. In the distance, behind the dome of the Co-op building, can be seen St. John's church.

(*Right*) A fine view of the junction of Broadgate, Hertford Street and Smithford Street around 1931. The bank on the left is now the only surviving building from this scene. Dunn and Co. occupies what became known as 'Dunn's corner' in the lower corner of the Kings Head Hotel. The Kings Head (Inn) first stood in Smithford Street from the 15th century. The old inn was demolished in the late 1870's and these larger premises opened as the Kings Head Hotel during Christmas 1879. This was Coventry's premier hotel, richly ornamented and equipped with Chippendale and Sheraton furniture. From his specially constructed 4th floor niche, Peeping Tom watched the world go by.

(*Right*) Looking west up Jordan Well towards Earl Street in 1929. The policeman is performing point duty at the junction with Cox, Gosford and Whitefriars streets. Beyond the Home & Colonial Stores lies the entrance to Freeth Street and above it a group of ancient timber buildings still stand hidden under bricks and plaster. These buildings survived the blitz but fell to the bulldozers in the early sixties. Further up the road can be seen the tower of the Council House in Earl street, the only identifiable landmark still remaining. The building jutting out on the left is again ancient, probably 16th century; that too was demolished to make way for the present Odeon Cinema.

(*Left*) Hundreds of school children gather at Pool Meadow on Easter Monday in 1929 for the Sunday Schools Procession. Every year on this day children from all over the city and its suburbs carried their Sunday School banners around the city watched by admiring parents and family. One person recalled that in the Meadow there was, 'singing of hymns, accompanied by massed bands.....The singing over, we would leave the Meadow in pre-arranged order to walk round the city streets.' The streets were lined with people and 'many would pass us oranges, biscuits, sweets and buns as we marched along.' After the procession a service was held at the Corn Exchange in Hertford Street. It is said that the last Sunday School Procession took place in 1940 when all the children carried their gas masks.

(*Right*) Looking west up Bayley Lane on a bright summer morning in 1930. On the right are the early English pillars of the South Porch of St. Michael's. This is the site of the first chapel. Opposite stands St. Mary's Guild Hall and the old wooden pump which may date to the 18th century. Number 22 Bayley Lane shows its fine carved barge-boards and latticed windows and of course its excellent carved corner post. Beyond the gothic mini-spire marks the site of St. Michael's Baptist Church which was destroyed in 1940 and afterwards used as a static water tank. It is now the site of the Newt and Cucumber Public House. Beyond the car is the Governors House, part of the old County Hall and Coventry Gaol.

(*Left*) In 1931 work got underway in Warwick Lane to clear the ground to build a new home for the Wesleyan movement whose congregation had outgrown their small chapel in Warwick Lane. The new Central Methodist Hall was built on ground once occupied by the friary of Greyfriars, in fact much of the building was erected on the extinct burial ground of this once well patronised house. John Shelton excavated the site and apart from discovering the long gone church's north transept, unearthed a six foot high wall and numerous human remains; remains of the Franciscan monks and more notable characters who were buried within the grounds. Shelton discovered two skulls encased in clay; these no doubt were the heads of Sir Henry Mumford and Sir Thomas Mallory who were sent to Coventry to be beheaded for treason. The deed was done under Binley Gallows, the site of the present Craven Arms, and their noble heads were used to decorate the city gates. Their bodies were taken by the Franciscans and interred in their graveyard and no doubt later the monks also acquired their heads. The remains depicted in the photographs are unknown but chances are he was a monk of the Franciscan order of the Greyfriars who dedicated his life to God with prayer and scholarship before finally being buried in a rough woollen shroud amongst his brethren. Of his fate in the modern world a plaque was placed on the east wall of Central Hall which read:

This pillar is attached to the north transept of the remains of the Greyfriars Church

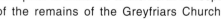

discovered during excavations.
 Beneath this window are re-interred the remains of the Greyfriars discovered during excavations. This building was opened in January 1932.

(*Above*) Laying the foundation stone of the Central Hall on a wet day in 1931. The hall was designed and built by Coventrians at a total cost of £40,000; £25,000 of which was given by an anonymous donor.

(*Right*) The Burges in 1932. The right-hand-side appears to have changed little to this day apart from the loss of original Victorian shop fronts. The first two shops are advertising Pork Pies, quality corn beef and Canterbury Lamb. Below can be seen the clock which is still an essential landmark in the Burges today. The two trams running on the double track served Broadgate to Broad Street via the Stoney Stanton Road. The large building (left, background) was Fearis & Company Provision Merchants which marked the beginning of Well Street.

(*Left*) The number 8, Earlsdon to Stoke (Bulls Head) tram stops outside the Opera House in Hales Street in 1932.

(*Below*) Looking south up Broadgate in 1932. Dominating the scene is the National Provincial Bank (now National Westminster) built in 1929/30. Behind it can be seen the Post Office and a single tram soon to be phased out in Hertford Street. The shops on the right are Burtons and John Astley & Sons, seed merchants and oil and glass merchants. On the left are Whitfield's, ladies tailors; Flinn & Co., silversmiths; Hayward & Sons, outfitters; Broadgate Café; Newtons; J. Lyons & Co., Café; T. Burbidge & Sons, Printers including Coventry Standard and Kenilworth Advertiser offices; Kendall & Sons, umbrella makers; The City Shirt Shop, and Salmon & Gluckstein, tobacconists.

(*Right*) Greyfriars Green in 1932, well wooded, neat and trim. Unlike the earlier photographs, this one shows the tower of the newly opened Central Methodist Hall in Warwick Lane (between the spires of Trinity on the left and St. Michael on the right).

(*Below*) A party of very respectable gentlemen stroll down Warwick Row to the Central Hall for its official opening ceremony on the 14th January 1932. This was a dream come true for the Wesleyans in Coventry; a group who began life in a small room at the rear of the market house in the 18th century, then later moved to a small chapel in Warwick Lane. Their founder John Wesley preached in the city three times in 1779, 1782 and 1786. On his first visit he was refused use of St. Mary's Hall in preference to a dancing master and because it was raining heavily was forced to preach from under cover of the market house. On a later visit an apology was given for this snub. We see in the photograph the Mayor, Alderman Vincent Wyles and the President of the Wesleyan Church, Dr. C. Ryder-Smith, leading the procession which, 'assembled at Warwick Road Congregational Church and marched to Warwick Lane, were Mrs. Morcome Taylor unlocked the main entrance. Then followed the dedicatory service, after the mayor had given a civic greeting, and at which the dedicatory address was given by the Rev. John Hornabrook.' Behind the procession can be seen the Rover Company car showrooms, which was later rebuilt as Benley's.

(*Right*) Looking up Hertford Street and Warwick Lane in 1933 (see map opposite). On the left at the corner of Bull Yard, stands the Peeping Tom public house (formerly the Railway Inn) the landlord of which was one Thomas Tudman. In its upper storey window can be seen a head and shoulders copy of Peeping Tom; this now can be seen at the top of Hertford Street. Above it another pub sign can be seen this was the Kenilworth Castle which stood next to popular Geisha Café. Above Curtis & Beamish on the right can be seen Luckmans Pianoforte Dealers this building still stands to this day bearing the companies name.

(*Left*) A fine view looking south up Broadgate to the National Provincial Bank in 1935. Notice the line of the bank building and Post Office as it curves down Hertford Street; a feature lost in the 1950's with the building of Broadgate House. Motor traffic is beginning to increase and there was much talk about dropping the tram system and converting solely to buses. At this time a doctored photograph appeared in the press showing how Broadgate would look minus the unsightly tram power lines so well portrayed in this photograph.

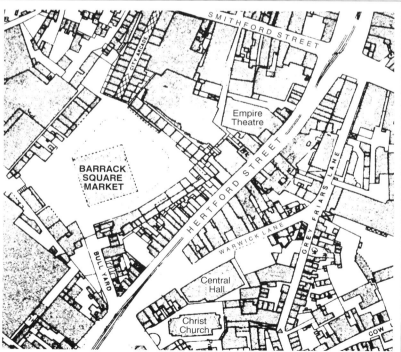

(*Above*) An unusual view looking up the Burges and Cross Cheaping in 1935. On the right stands The Wine Lodge built in 1932. Later names are The Tally Ho and now the Tudor Rose. Note how the buildings higher up follow the original line of the street. These would later be demolished and re-aligned with the lower buildings. On the left can be seen Glenn & Co., tobacconist and confectioner; Wyles Footwear; John Hough's, home of the celebrated Hough's Pork Pies (John Hough founded a mission for poor children) and Gilbert & Sons, jewellers. This is now Louisa James, jewellers and retains its beautiful original Victorian Art Nouvea façade and of course its clock. This constitutes the finest surviving shop front in the city.

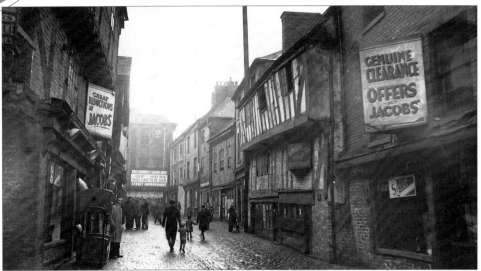

(*Below*) The same view as the last but a little further up shows more demolition signs. William Franks, a long time furnishing trader, informs the public of his move to Fleet Street. The sign on the shoe warehouse which formed the south end of Broadgate ironically declares, 'This Corner to be Taken Away Street Improvements.' We all can now see the great potential of streets such as this, as those at York and Chester testify.

(*Right*) An earlier picture facing north in happier times, a reminder of a past lost and an opportunity missed. Half way down on the right can be seen Moore's Oyster Bar better known today as Fishy Moores.

(*Above*) Looking south up a wet Great Butcher Row in November 1935. In 1910 Alderman Vincent Wyles put forward a plan to open up the city centre for increasing road traffic. This plan included the demolition of some of Coventry's finest surviving medieval streets, namely Great and Little Butcher Rows, Bullring, Ironmonger Row, Cross Cheaping and part of New Buildings. This plan faced much opposition and never got off the ground. It did however come to fruition on New Years Day 1936 when Butcher Row was officially closed by Alderman C. Payne before a small group of people. The plan was to build Vincent Wyles' vision and call it Trinity Street. Once again there was much opposition and alternative plans put forward but the destruction went ahead. This photograph taken by the entrance to Priory Row shows many of the shops bearing closing down signs. Jacobs Furnishings offering 'Great Reductions' and on the right the sign of A.W. Garlick, which had hung there for nearly half a century, looks grimey. The shop, previously that of a hatter in the days of top hats, stands forlorn awaiting the inevitable.

The destruction begins early in 1936 photographed from the tower of Holy Trinity Church. More than 500 years of Coventry's past is wiped away; in the foreground can be seen the rear of the houses in Butcher Row these made up a lane much favoured by artists and was called Trinity Lane. It is now the cobbled roadway in front of Trinity church. In the middle, running from left to right, can be seen the bottom of Broadgate and Cross Cheaping, all of this section in the foreground was to fall, and more..........

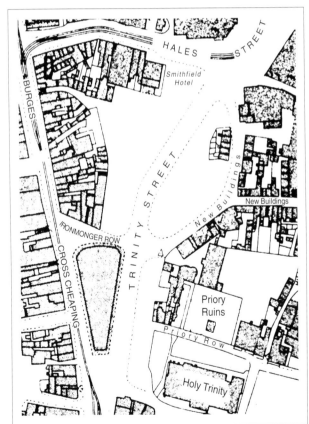

(*Left*) The beauty of this view lies in the churches, all else is barbarous vandalism in the first degree. The area is once again an open square as it was in the early days of long gone Coventry Priory. The three-storied timbered building awaiting destruction marks the corner of Priory Row and back from it (left) can be seen the cottage which thankfully survived the destruction. The digger on the right is standing on the edge of a 30 foot deep sandstone quarry which contained rubbish. In the upper levels were 14th century objects and at the very bottom the remains of a small pony. Above that was the cellar of a medieval house, 20 foot deep and cut out of solid rock. The timber building in the background also had a fine vaulted 14th century cellar and the whole area was covered with cellars which caused the developers many problems. Many objects of historic interest were brought to light mainly by J. B. Shelton, who worked flat out to rescue and record what he could.

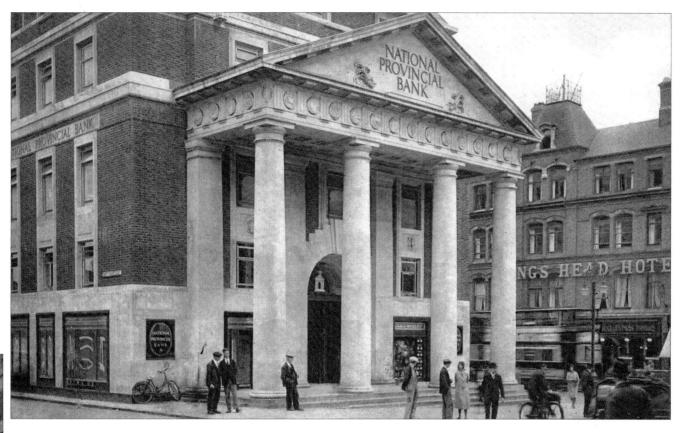

(*Left*) Looking from Hertford Street down Broadgate in 1936. The top of Cross Cheaping is fenced off and bears a sign reading William Tomkinson & Son, Contractors who are working below in the Trinity Street construction. It appears to be a Sunday and, according to the Broadgate clock, nearly ten fifteen. All the shops are closed except for Salmon & Gluckstein's the tobacconists on the corner of Broadgate and the High Street. Hiltons Boot & Shoe Store at the bottom is still standing but not for long. On the right, in the Bank Chambers, is James Walker, jeweller which recently occupied this corner. From this angle Broadgate truly lives up to its name.

(*Above*) The National Provincial Bank dominates Broadgate in 1936. This is perhaps one of Coventry's most important pre-war buildings and deserved to be given a second glance. Built between 1929/30 it is based on Classical Greek and Roman architecture and bears Roman columns facing Broadgate and Greek in Hertford Street. The building is decorated with copies of Greek coins and these can be seen over the entrance, on the fine metal door and inside the building. The Broadgate entrance is meant to resemble the entrance to a Roman temple such as the temple of Claudius which stood in Colchester. The interior of the building has some nice touches including an unusual thick glass skylight. Opposite stands the King's Head Hotel, Coventry's premier hotel.

(*Below*) Broadgate in May 1937 decorated for the coronation of King George VI. A lorry leaves the construction site from behind the fence as Trinity Street nears completion. Note the two Daimler buses (originally purchased in 1933); the one in the middle of Broadgate is the number 6 to Earlsdon. Trams, led by the number 5 to Bell Green, await fares by the inspectors

(*Centre*) An unusual view of Hertford Street from the roof of the National Provincial Bank in 1936. On the right is the end of the King's Head and the entrance to its private car park. Next is the tobacconist and sweet shop and below that the Empire Cinema

hut opposite Market Place and Boots the Chemist. The tram system was on its way out for in this year trams to Gosford Green, Earlsdon and Coventry Station were replaced by buses.

(formerly the Corn Exchange). In the distance by the Bull Yard can be seen the showrooms of Rover Cars. On the left, next to the bank, stands the Central Post Office which is shown four stories high but has since lost its top floor.

Next to it is the small and select Queen's Hotel; it was from here in 1896 that the Mayor with six policeman deliberately broke the law by riding with Leon Bollee on his petroleum tandem. The vehicle was illegal because it moved over four miles per 14th blitz. Hertford Street remained in use as a passable road into the late 1960's when it was closed and pedestrianised.

(*Below*) Trinity Street was officially opened on the 16th September 1937 at a total cost of £260,400. Here Mayor Alderman Barnacle is seen addressing the crowds

hour and this was against the Red Flag Act which stated that any vehicle capable of over four miles per hour should be preceded by a man carrying a red flag. The Queen's was blown up in an attempt to stop fire spreading to the Post Office during the November before officially cutting the ribbon which was stretched across the road. After the ribbon was cut the official group, followed by many spectators, walked to the bottom of Trinity Street where Alderman Barnacle handed the ceremonial scissors to ex-mayor Alderman Vincent Wyles who envisaged the street in 1910. Alderman Wyles then cut the second ribbon officially opening the whole street.

(*Right*) A driver stands opposite Market Place in Broadgate, he is waiting beside his Bedworth tram for the appointed time to leave. Behind can be seen newly opened Trinity Street stretching down to the new Hippodrome which was opened in November 1937. Note to the right of it still stands the old Hippodrome built in 1906; this was soon to be demolished and Lady Herbert's Garden extended onto the site. The left hand-side of the street, including the first Owen Owen Department Store, has been opened but the right-hand side still awaits development.

(*Below*) An excellent view taken from the High Street side of Greyfriars Lane in 1937 looking towards Smithford Street and Broadgate. On the left stands the King's Head Hotel minus its figure of Peeping Tom in the top corner window. The figure was now standing in the hotel hallway. On the right stands the Burton's building and around the corner Wilsons Ladies clothing. Above both of these stores the second floor served as the Venetian Café and the third floor at this time was to let. As always a white helmeted policeman stands on point duty at the cross roads directing the Daimler bus to it destination, Stoke Heath.

(*Above*) Cross Cheaping and the Burges in 1937. On the right stands the newly opened Owen Owen Store and left can be seen old Cross Cheaping consisting mainly of Victorian and early 20th century buildings. The exception is George Mason, grocers and Franks the optician. Beneath its plaster is a three-storied 16th century timbered merchants house, once one of the finer properties of the period. Opposite was once the entrance to Little Butcher Row. The premises below Owens on the right are unchanged to this day; also buildings at the bottom left side of the Burges have survived. Note in the distance how high the land rises up Bishop Street.

(*Above*) This excellent photograph was taken from the roof of the Gas Showrooms in Corporation Street in 1937. The white building on the right, now Belgrade Square, stands on the corner of Fretton Street (now Upper Well Street) and in the background can be seen St. John's. Despite the fact that the land on the right was cleared in 1930 it still stands vacant after seven years. On the left, with a seating capacity of 2,550, stands the Rex Cinema opened 8th February 1937 by the mayor Alderman Barnacle. This was one of the country's most prestigious cinema's. Designed by architect Robert Cromie it was lavish Art Deco style and had a copper-faced pay box with decorative steel bands. The plush pastel red auditorium faced stage curtains of pink and silver and the cinema's Café was decorated floor to ceiling with a jungle scene, reflective glass-like pillars and an aviary as its centrepiece. At the time this photograph was taken the Rex was showing 'The General Died at Dawn'. Sadly Coventry's newest and most lavish cinema was hit by a very large bomb on Sunday night, 25th August 1940. This bomb flattened the building sending its front doors flying through the air and eventually landing in Gas Street. Staff who turned up for work the following morning were shocked, including the owner and director who were both discovered close to tears in what was originally the foyer. Ironically the next film scheduled to be shown on that day was the great classic 'Gone with the Wind.' There was talk at the time of rebuilding but that was put to an end when the remains of the building were hit again in October. The site was later cleared and became the home of the Rex Market up until the 1950's.

(*Right*) A fine view from Broadgate of Cross Cheaping and Trinity Street in 1938. In the centre of the two roads stands Coventry's first Owen Owen Department Store opened in 1937.

(*Below*) A more detailed view of Trinity Street taken in 1938. Owen Owen has been trading for sometime and below the new shops and offices are nearing completion. On the right can be seen what will soon become the familiar flower bed following the line of Butcher Row. The area below awaits the building of shops advertised with upper room accommodation as required.

(*Right*) A photograph taken from the tower of St. Michael's in 1938 looking down on Trinity Street.

Beyond Holy Trinity can be seen Owen Owen now sporting a new sign on its frontage. Below lies the lower part of the street, not quite completed and, except for a change in roof level, still unchanged to this day. At the top of this building which stands in Ironmonger Row, can still be seen the entrance to Palmer Lane. On this corner originally stood the Pilgrim's Rest, a guest house for pilgrims visiting the nearby Priory. The entrance stood across the road by the fenced area, now outside H. Samuel's the Jeweller. Behind the Owen's building still stands a large factory called the Victoria Work's or 'Paddy's Folly.' It was built as a weaving factory in 1860

by Irishman James Hart of Copsewood Grange. Sadly he could not foresee the collapse of the industry the following year and despite winning national awards for his ribbons in 1862 was made bankrupt and had to sell the factory and his home. Later the factory was acquired by the Rover and Centaur cycle companies. Driven by steam power, Rover used the first, third and fourth floors while Centaur used the second floor. On the right of Trinity church can be seen Blue Coat School and the old wooden bell campanile which held the bells of Trinity from 1855 to the 1960's. It is said when these bells were rung to celebrate the end of the Crimean war the tower lurched from side to side and roof tiles fell off much to the consternation of the bell ringers who had to run for their lives. Not surprisingly the tower was reinforced.

(*Above*) The number 8 tram from Earlsdon to the Bulls Head at Stoke rattles up Vernon Street into Paynes Lane. This route ran from 1899 to 1940 and included Hales Street, White Street, Victoria Street, King William Street, Vernon Street, Paynes Lane and the Binley Road. Trams were now coming to an end in the city as more routes were taken over by buses. During 1937 routes from Broadgate to Gosford Green; Earlsdon to Broadgate and Coventry Station to Broadgate were discontinued. It was planned to scrap the whole system by 1942 at the latest.

(*Right*) An atmospheric night time shot of trams in Broadgate taken by city photographer James Armer whose photographic shop stood for over sixty years on the Stoney Stanton Road. James took this shot with a plate camera on a tripod. The tram inspector stopped the two trams so James could capture them for prosperity.

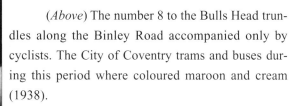

(*Above*) The number 8 to the Bulls Head trundles along the Binley Road accompanied only by cyclists. The City of Coventry trams and buses during this period where coloured maroon and cream (1938).

(*Right*) A very pleasant and quiet Leamington Road as it looked in the summer of 1938. At the end of the road can be seen the old Styvechale Tollgate built in the 18th century and demolished against public opinion in 1964. This toll house controlled the traffic on these toll-roads (also the Kenilworth Road) with two white gates which allowed access only to those who paid the appropriate fee. These gates were removed in 1872 due to the Toll House Removal Act.

(*Below*) Construction of Whites the Chemist begins against the 17th century cottage in Priory Row late in 1938. On the right the flower bed, which lines present Trinity Street, is half constructed. During this work, which involved underpinning Blue Coat School (left),

a number of skeletons were discovered. The Coventry Herald reported: *The bones were found huddled against an old stone wall which had lain buried for hundreds of years. Their position suggested that the bodies of which they had once formed the framework had been buried* *together, while cleavages of the skulls of several of them appeared to have been caused during lifetime and not since the burial of the bodies. Mr. J. B. Shelton, the well known Coventry antiquary, who has examined them, offers a probable explanation. He recalls that there were many battles and skirmishes in the environs of Coventry. The splendid condition of the teeth in the skulls causes him to take the view that the skeletons were those of young men......killed in battle.......it is thought that the skeletons are probably about 700 years old. This discovery was made close to various sections of the 13th century Cathedral of St. Mary which are being unearthed almost hour by hour in the course of the excavations for a big block of shops and business premises.......Unfortunately, the building operations now proceeding do not admit of the latest discoveries being preserved. Consequently, as these relics of the cathedral ruins are found, they are having to be removed.* It is most likely that these young men who died mainly from sword wounds to the head were probably associated with Earl Marmion of Tamworth who came to Coventry in 1143 to take Coventry Castle. He and his knights drove the monks from the priory and fortified it. Marmion was decapitated by a common soldier after falling into one of his own fortification ditches. There is no record of how much force Marmion, known as a 'man great in warr' used to drive the monks away. Sword wounds to the head suggest they may not have been soldiers because even common foot troops wore helmets perfectly capable of deflecting sword blows. Whoever these unfortunate young men were they were reburied in nearby Trinity Churchyard.

(*Centre*) The spires of Holy Trinity and St. Michael dominate the skyline in this photograph taken early in 1939. The flower bed is nearly completed in Trinity Street and the steps are being added from Priory Row. The graveyard of Trinity has been tidied up and many of the gravestones moved. During construction of the street in 1936 Shelton noted in the Austin Monthly Magazine that, ' Human remains were unearthed at the top of Butcher Row,' adding simply, 'These were re-interred near the spot where they were found.'

(*Right*) A photograph taken on 30th May 1939 of trams in their shed at the Priestley Bridge Depot on the Stoney Stanton Road. This depot

began life as an electricity generating plant for the new electric tram system introduced in 1895. To generate this power it used coal supplied by the local Wyken and Walsgrave pits. In 1899 the generating works was extended by the Coventry Electric Tramways Company to include the systems main repairs centre. By 1913 Coventry Corporation extended it again this time serving

as the city's main tram depot. At this time there were only five tram routes in use, these were to Earlsdon, Coventry Station, Stoke, Bell Green and Bedworth.

(*Below*) The Earl Street end of Little Park Street in 1939. A lorry rumbles past the Miners Union Club, a building which for many years since has stood empty despite being one of the finest period Georgian houses in the country. The original narrowness of the street can be seen, a feature which would have been familiar to the Coventry Martyrs whose last steps taken in Coventry was in this street. Joan Ward, Mrs. Smith, Thomas Lansdail, Hawkins, Wrigsham, Robert Hockett, Thomas Bond, Robert Silksby, Laurence Saunders, Robert Glover and Cornelius Bongey were all burnt to death at the stake for their beliefs. The execution was carried out in the 'Park Hollows' in the Little Park.

(*Centre*) Looking halfway down the chancel and nave of St. Michael's one year before its destruction. The central area was opened up by replacing the Victorian pews with chairs. As war loomed the medieval stain glass was taken out from the aspe and clerestory before

being taken out of the city and stored at Hampton Lucy. Near the altar hung the Union Flag and the colours of the Royal Warwickshire Regiment, these were rescued as the building burned during the blitz. Restoration work later revealed a rare 14th century pardon brass hidden beneath the Victorian floor. Little evidence remained telling to which knight it was dedicated but whoever prayed for him would receive 20 days pardon. No other old brasses remained in the church following the visit, during the Reformation, of a man bearing a false commission to remove such objects. It is also noticeable that Trinity's brasses before this period are also missing.

(*Right*) A beautiful photograph looking up the nave of St. Michael's towards the west door and tower through to the north aisle into St. Andrew's Chapel. Light streams through the upper windows beneath the 100 foot high hammer-beam medieval roof. At the base of the tower and above a board carrying a list of vicars, is a life size figure of St. Michael carved, painted and gilded by artist Alec Miller of Chipping Campden. The Cathedral church contained many other works of art and monuments which told the history of Coventry. These included the wonderful tomb of Elizabeth Swillington; her image lay between her two husbands, one in armour and the other in robe and chain of office of Coventry's Recorder. It bore the inscription (in Latin), *Pray for the soul of Elizabeth Swillington, widow, late the wife of Ralph Swillington, Attorney General of our Lord King Henry VIII, Recorder of the city of Coventry, formerly the wife of Thomas Essex Esq: which said Elizabeth died A.D. 15??* (after 1543). The altar tomb of city mayor Julian Nethermyl stood through the piers in the top of the north aisle. This fine Italianate marble tomb had on its front a crucifix, words of dedication and the arms of the Nethermyl's. On the left-hand side of this could be seen Julian Nethermyl and his five sons kneeling in prayer and on the right his wife and five daughters doing likewise. Above this was a brass to the memory of Mary Hinton, wife of the vicar, who died in 1594. She was shown kneeling in prayer be-

fore four babies in swaddling on the ground, suggesting she lost all four when but babes. These are but three of the dozens of memorials now lost from the cathedral. Note

on the photograph how the tower is out of line with the main body of the church and how the roof was raised in medieval times when the nave was enlarged. The tall tower arch shows the original height and narrowness of the church's earlier structure. The west door may have been built or rebuilt in 1451 to form a grand entrance for King Henry VI when he and his court attended high mass before granting the city the status of the County of the City of Coventry.

(*Below*) Looking across the nave and north aisle into St. Andrews Chapel (old Smith's Chapel) and the Girdler's Chapel. St. Andrew's Chapel (left) was founded by the Guild of Smiths around 1449 and the Girdler's Chapel (right) was founded in 1390 and originally dedicated to All Saints. These particular chapels are however not the originals for these outer aisles where not built before 1500. Right of the woman enjoying the tranquillity in the outer north aisle, can be seen a small doorway which led to an external pulpit and the roof. Next to this, but obscured, is the north porch entrance, now gone.

(*Right*) A busy Broadgate at 6.50am in 1939. The number 5 to Bell Green waits by the inspectors hut opposite Market Place and the number 8 to Stoke pulls in behind it. The newspaper sellers sign (right) bears the message, 'Lords Rush Through I.R.A. Bill.' This refers to a terrorism bill passed due to I.R.A. bombings on the mainland which began in February 1939. Coventrians too were to suffer after a number of explosive devices went off around the city. Five were killed and dozens injured in Broadgate when a bomb in a cycle basket blew up outside Astley's (near Burtons) on 25th August 1939. The bicycle was leant against the post box next to the Keresley bus stop. Five were arrested and two found guilty who paid with their own lives.

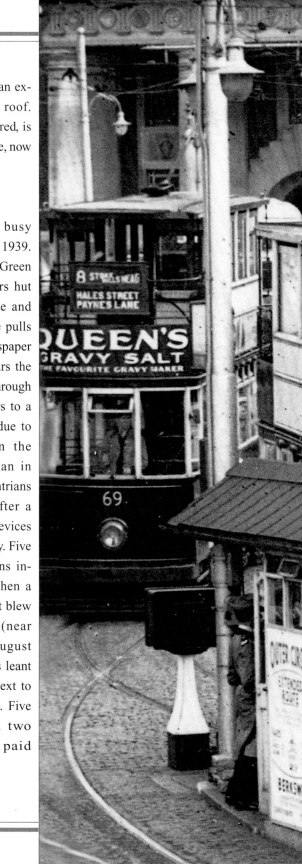

(*Left*) Looking down Market Street from Smithford Street late in 1939. War has been declared and people can be seen carrying gas masks. Many stopped carrying them after the 'Phoney War' officially ended and the Battle of Britain began. On the corner is Spalls, sellers of fancy goods and for many years familiar in the centre of Coventry. Next door is Glieberman's furriers; William Cleverley seller of hats and on the corner the Lamp Tavern. This is the birthplace of England's greatest Edwardian actress Dame Ellen Terry born on February 27th 1847. The actual building she was born in has, since her fame, caused much controversy. Some have said it was on the west side and others on the east side. When Dame Ellen came to the city in 1906 to lay a commemorative stone at the former Corn Exchange she was asked by the editor of the Coventry Standard about her birthplace and said: "My dear mother used to say, you go into Market Street and the house is on the right-hand side." When asked which end of Market Street she laughed, knowing the controversy, and said: "Don't ask me to attempt to settle that. That way madness lies." She was then told by the editor that he believed her birthplace was number 5, to which she replied laughingly, "Number five forever." At that time two buildings bore plaques claiming to be the birthplace one a haberdashers and the other a tripe shop which stood opposite. It is generally now agreed that Number 5, the haberdashers, was the correct building.

(*Right*) A fine view looking up Hertford Street in 1939. On the right can be seen the offices of the Birmingham Post and Mail advertising the fact that 'British Pledges Anger Germany.' Next door stands Odell's estate agents advertising, as sold, a freehold residence in Finham called 'Crossways.' Next is Piquerez; Madame Piquerez' hairdressing and beauty salon and beyond Johnson & Masons who once owned a warehouse and

shop taking up the whole length of the bank and post office. Onward down the street is Patterson's, British School of Motoring, Pearl Assurance and the Queen's Hotel. All awaiting destruction in the next fateful year.

(*Above*) One of the last ever Christmas's for old Coventry in the late 1930's. Soon things would change forever and Coventry would never be the same again. The tree awaits its lights and Broadgate its decorations. The Riley Kestrel (left of the tram) which is parked outside Boots the Chemist will soon itself be wrecked in the bombing of November 14th 1940 and will later be rebuilt at the Riley factory. Leading up to Christmas old Coventry thronged with shoppers as late night shopping was allowed. The city was also full of church goers and celebrators on Christmas Eve.

'Your Courage, Your Cheerfulness, Your Resolution, Will Bring Us Victory.'

(*Below*) The time is one minute to eleven o'clock; the date is November the 11th 1940, everything grinds to a halt as St. Michael's bells are about to toll the eleventh hour in memory of the dead of the Great War and the new war. Notice all face Broadgate; men with caps in hand awaiting the hour. Here in the centre of Coventry and throughout the land everything will stop dead for two minutes of remembrance. Little did anyone realise just how long and how devastating to this city this new war would be. Black out regulations are now taking effect as all the vehicles have hoods over their headlights, some also have white paint on their bumpers and running boards as another officially recommended precaution. This view is of the east side of Broadgate

(*Above*) Looking up Smithford Street from an upper storey window of the City Arcade in 1940. Both the Arcade, Woolworth's and British Home Stores opposite were built further back from the original street line in accordance with a plan begun in 1936 to rebuild Smithford Street. The tram lines can still be seen in the cobbled street although trams stopped running up here in 1932. On this busy Saturday afternoon with hardly anyone bothering to carry a gas mask, there is little to suggest a war is on. However, the clues are hidden within the picture including signs for an air raid shelter capable of holding 330 people. Also on the horse-drawn vehicle from the railway station is a sign of official encouragement reading:

heading up towards the corner of High Street which now lies under Cathedral Lanes.

(*Below*) This photograph looking across the corner of Broadgate and down the High Street was taken at the same time as the previous picture. The vehicles on this side have yet to comply with the new blackout regulations, although the lorry appears to have one light covered in cloth and white paint on the corners of its front rims. Much of the High Street survived the war except for its only two Elizabethan buildings. After being lovingly restored in 1936 they took a direct hit in November 1940. On the right can be seen the National Bank (then Lloyds Bank) built like some great mausoleum around 1933. Next is Waters of Coventry which traded

from 1802 until 1991. The mock Tudor style timbered building is the Craven Arms rebuilt in 1914. The original inn was itself Tudor and began life as the White Bear.

(*Above*) With war came the need for civil defence such as air-raid wardens, auxiliary fire service and home guard. Here we have a group of Coventry Auxiliary Fire Service men and women at their headquarters somewhere in Coventry enjoying the simple things in life – tea, bread and Kraft cheese. Note the blackout curtains in the background.

(*Right*) These are the Auxiliary Fire Service lads of Station 605 based at the London Laundry and photographed in 1940. They served the Stoney Stanton Road area which was known locally as 'Hellfire Corner,' because of the bombs which regularly fell there. After a days work they were into uniform and straight down the station where they spent the night. The stations sub-officer Bill Boucher recalls that the men of 605 were involved in every raid on the city and recalled that one of the men, Syd Buckler, used to work until seven, cycle home to Ryton have his dinner and report for duty every night at eight. Despite this he got a warning from the Home Office about his timekeeping. Syd was remembered as always being

cheerful and a tower of strength when the bombs were falling. During a raid in April Syd was killed as he ushered people into an air raid shelter while telling them not to worry. Two other 605 men died with him, brothers Ivor and Albert. One night the station itself was destroyed and the fire fighters based themselves in what remained of one of their houses.

(*Left*) One of 605 station was known as 'Cheerful Charlie' because he had an infectious grin. Looking at the lads relaxing on their converted Hillman Minx they all appear to be cheerful. Underlying these smiling faces were men determined to do their duty at all cost. With a steadfast resolve they worked for the war effort during the day and gave all their other time for the protection of neighbours. Notice in the background the church (now closed) on the Stoney Stanton Road.

'COVENTRATED'
The death of old Coventry

With the outbreak of war Coventry became an important centre for war production and the population swelled with imported war workers. The city's mechanised industries, which began in the 1860's, would inadvertently lead to Coventry's destruction as they became important targets to stem the flow of planes, military vehicles and munitions. The earliest attacks on the city and its surrounds began on June 25th 1940 when five bombs were dropped on Ansty Aerodrome and two days later bombs fell on Hillfields killing 16 people. The heaviest raid of the period was on the 25th August when the Rex cinema was destroyed. Between then and the end of October the city suffered a further 16 raids resulting in 176 deaths and the temporary destruction of Fords Hospital. At the beginning of November bombers visited the city 7 times but did little damage. These were but minor seemingly uncoordinated raids but worst was to come. Hitler was infuriated after the RAF bombed Munich, the birthplace of his Nazi movement, and yearned for revenge; operation Moonlight Sonata was instigated. Five hundred bombers were gathered and during the early evening of November 14th 1940 the Squadron leader of one group told his men, "Our task is, with other squadrons, to repay the attack on Munich by the English during the night of 8th November. We shall not repay it in the same manner by smashing up harmless dwelling houses, but we shall do it in such a way that those over there will be completely stunned. Even though the attack on Munich by the gentlemen of the Royal Air Force was a complete failure, neither the Fuehrer nor our Commander-in-Chief, Reichsmarschall Goring is willing to let even the attempt at an attack on the capital of the movement go unpunished, and we have therefore received orders to destroy the industries of Coventry tonight." Each squadron was given its target, consisting of the Standard works, the Coventry Radiator and Press Company, the Alvis works, the British Piston Ring Company, the Daimler works and the gas holder in Hill Street. The factories were not the only targets, for despite the claim that civilians were not being attacked, Coventry was to be obliterated 'Coventrated' (as the Germans called it) wiped off the face of the earth. The attack was led by a special pathfinder unit called Kampfgeschwader 100 who followed set radio beams called X-Gerat to their target. These beams were being jammed from England but were unfortunately on the wrong frequency pitch making the jamming totally ineffective. There was much confusion at this time as a large raid was expected in England during the full moon period but nobody knew for sure when or where. Some have suggested that Churchill knew of the raid in advance and sacrificed the city to hide from the Germans the fact that we had cracked their Enigma code. This is wrong for on that November afternoon Churchill was on his way to Ditchley House in Oxfordshire and while travelling opened his high security messages; one informed him that the big raid was to be that night although the target was still unspecified. Churchill, like many others, assumed it was to be London and ordered the driver to take him back. On arriving in Downing Street he ordered his secretaries into the shelter and, as was his custom, went onto the roof of the Air Ministry and awaited the raid that never came. Later, as other intelligence reached him, he knew better. Meanwhile in Coventry, underneath the Post Office in Hertford Street, streams of planes were being tracked in the War Operations Room. Soon at around 7 o'clock a droning sound could be heard in the distance quickly followed by the eerie but now familiar wail of the air raid siren. The moon was full and bright lighting up the city and a westerly breeze blew. At 7.20pm the pathfinder squadron reached the city and began dropping parachute flares which hung in the sky followed by exploding incendiaries. These were the markers, starting fires and opening up targets for the following incessant stream of bombers. Amid the drone of the planes and swishings of falling incendiaries could be heard the thunderous roar of the ack-ack and Bofur guns. Soon fires were burning everywhere, at the cathedral, in Broadgate, all around; screams from the air heralded the dropping of high explosives and buildings shook and were blasted apart as they hit home. By 7.40pm the cathedral was being engulfed in flames, as was the city. The emergency services were fighting an ever losing battle as fire took hold and no water was available as bombs had burst the mains. Water was pumped from the Sherbourne, Coventry canal and the Swanswell but as soon as pipes were laid they were broken again. One out of town group of firemen disappeared in one explosion while laying pipes from the Swanswell. By 2.0am Coventry was engulfed by at least 200 fires, with red flames roaring up to a 100 feet into the sky; the bombers could see their target just after crossing the channel. Nonstop they came hour after long hour, the city centre aflame as incendiaries continued to make their familiar swishing sound as they fell. High explosives screamed down blasting the city apart and raining shrapnel everywhere. Occasionally a large iron box, suspended by a parachute (land-mine), would slowly fall and with a horrendous

blast would lay flat any building near it. It was as if the bowels of hell had burst forth upon the city. One hotel owner later told of his experiences that night: "When the sirens wailed, only my wife, daughter Mary and I were on duty. Within a few minutes incendiaries and bombs were screaming down; Mary decided to make for the shelter in Broadgate. I had placed valuables such as money and jewellery in a bag upstairs for safety. These were soon lost. The upper walls of the building collapsed and caught alight. It was impossible to get up the stairs. The only refuge we had was the cellar but eventually we had to leave it. The heat from the city, burning all about us, made it too hot to stay. For some time we couldn't get out because the entrance was blocked by burning timber and fallen stone and bricks. It wasn't until 1.30a.m. that by superhuman effort I heaved up the iron drop gates which led from the cellar into the hotel yard. We tried to escape from the crashing, burning building by running through the yard and along the passage which led to Broadgate. We were met by a river of burning butter and fat flowing from the Maypole (Dairy). It was terrifying! We rushed to escape through the burning hotel itself. The building was now just a heap of blazing ruins but we made it into Market Square. The roar of flames, the crash of bombs, the scorching heat made our positions seem hopeless! Yet we still aimed at getting through to Broadgate and the crash of a bursting petrol tank in a burning bus in Market Square lent speed to our feet. I shall never forget that awful dash for the shelter, leading my wife through masses of red-hot debris and fallen tramway wires. She had a tin basin on her head and I had an enamel bucket on mine. I'm sure that if we hadn't had these for protection we'd have been left without a hair on our heads." Those in the shelters did not always fare well, but courage shone through as this letter from Deputy Chief Warden Timms testifies. He writes of a shelter he was in charge of under Messrs O'Brien's in which people were killed. Telling what happened he writes: 'A delayed action bomb came through one end of the shelter, killing an elderly lady and injuring her daughter rather badly. Five other people were slightly injured . Then followed the finest show of bravery by a great number of British I shall be privileged to witness. Their courage will remain in my memory forever. When the bomb came through the shelters there were over 1,500 people packed in them. When we moved them as far as we could from the bomb evacuating half the shelter and packing them into a space that should hold about 300 people, you could not move in the passages for people packed in one huge mass.......All the lights went out and the shelters flooded with water. At the centre of the shelters is a large boiler, and with the water rising quickly those people knew it might explode at any moment. This on top of being within a few yards of a bomb that might explode any moment. These people, knowing all this did not show the least spark of fear or panic. Some sang, some joked, but not one complained. Would that some of the German people could see how hopeless it is for them to break the spirit of the British race. One elderly lady of 80 stood in water for six hours and said how she wished she had a cup of tea and her rubber boots. Another woman, who had left her bag in a cubicle through which the bomb came in, was told to keep away and we would fetch her bag for her. While we were elsewhere she went and got it herself, explaining to me when I told her she had been foolhardy, that she couldn't afford to lose it as she has 35 shillings in it. The children were magnificent; although they wanted a drink of water they never asked the second time when told there was none.' Outside this dark dank shelter bombs continued to fall killing many, one such was described by Howard Tomley a Civil Defence Staff Officer, he reported that, 'I proceeded along Jordan Well into Earl Street. There was a body of a youth lying on the pavement just underneath the Council House clock; he was dead. Later I heard he was one of the brave body of police messengers.' And so it went on for eleven long hours of death, destruction and bravery. One of the few remaining sirens wailed the all-clear at around 6.15am on the following morning. The Luftwaffe had unloaded 500 tons of high explosives, 30,000 incendiaries and 50 land mines on the city. Amongst the burning ruins and rubble lay 554 dead and 865 injured; 45,000 homes were destroyed and 75% of the city's industry damaged. That more had not died was something of a miracle and for many years rumours spread about cover-ups, but these were just rumours. The late Eric Bramwell, local historian, who was on watch in the council house most of the night wrote a short note on the morning of the 15th. It reads: 'Fires still burning, unchecked, all around the city centre, craters and rubble in the streets. The devastation is indescribable. Service personnel make their way slowly over the debris. No one speaks. My personal feeling is one of sadness. Then I recall the starling trilling a few notes of song as Entwhistle and I left the Council House this morning. Did the heat of the fires make the bird think it was spring, or could this be a message of hope for the future?' Truly old Coventry lay in ruins and Coventrians could only dream of a better future.

(*Above*) Fireman tackling the blazing top floor of the Queen's Hotel in Hertford Street November 15th. Behind can be seen the Post Office and bank, underneath which could be found the areas War Operations Headquarters.

(*Right*) Stunned Coventrians walk through Broadgate on the morning of November 15th. Despite knowing what had happened, many turned up for work only to find their place of work no longer existed. The city was overhung with a grey acrid smoke and fires continued to burn. Bodies, burnt and torn apart, lay scattered throughout the city's streets. Owen Owen was destroyed by incendiaries the previous evening; it had stood for only three years.

(*Above*) The bottom of Broadgate and the top of Cross Cheaping. People stand on the triangular pavement that stood before Owen Owen. On the left is the remains of the keep left sign and the site of the tram inspectors hut opposite Market Place. Despite the destruction and gloom a Union Jack flies.

(*Right*) Further down Cross Cheaping with Owen Owen on the right. The bus on the left is one of six which was destroyed; thirteen were badly damaged but rebuildable and thirty four had major damage. As for the tram system, tracks were found embedded in peoples house and in their back gardens and seen in some places distorted and bent 30 feet into the air. The tram system would need five months to rebuild, so it was scrapped.

(*Above*) A soldier stands in Jordan Well at the junction of Much Park Street. He is one of six hundred quickly brought in to maintain order, help search for bodies, blow up unsafe buildings and deal with some 280 unexploded bombs. One person wrote to his wife, 'Soldiers are everywhere, standing at ends of roads and streets with fixed bayonets, asking your business.' Coventry did not see proper daylight on the 15th as a black fog hung over the city all day. Note the shovel laying at the roadside as work quickly got underway to open up the main streets again to speed up the passage of aid to the city. In the background in Earl Street can be seen the clock tower of the Council House which suffered minor damage.

(*Above*) The smog had lifted on the 16th but fires still smouldered in the city. Much was underway to repair essential roads which were badly cratered and gas, electricity and water mains. Fresh water was brought in tankers and initially free food was supplied. Many shopkeepers set up in the ruins of their buildings and carried on as best they could. The Broadgate clock stopped at twenty one minutes to eleven as the east side of Broadgate was devastated by high explosives. In the background can be seen the tower and spire of Holy Trinity which miraculously suffered little damage.

(*Left*) Another view of Cross Cheaping 15th November. People all appear to have places to go and stare straight ahead as if nothing is unusual. However, one soldier stares at the photographer.

had been dealt with nothing on earth could have saved Coventry Library.' This part of the building was the reference section which contained thousands of valuable and rare books. It was later demolished and in the fifties became the Festival Cafe with outside seats and a tourist information hut. It now forms the back entrance to Cathedral Lanes and the site of the present Coventry Cross.

(*Below*) Looking down Cross Cheaping from what was Market Place. The Keresley bus is going nowhere. Coventry now had many orphans and homeless families in need of help and support. On the 16th November King George VI came to see the devastation for himself. In Eileen Castle's pamphlet *The City Under Fire*, she recalled this visit as remembered by an unspecified Coventrian who said: *I was in Hay Lane, by the corner of Anslows* [now Yates]. *There was a queue of people trying to get some news of relatives*

(*Above*) The Rev. Clitheroe of Holy Trinity wrote in his booklet *Coventry Under Fire*, 'after extinguishing the fire in the loft, we saw the City Library, which stood alongside the southern boundary wall, was alight. This too was lamentable, for we knew how precious were its contents, and how much they meant to us in Coventry........Once again, could we dare dash across? We had stores of water and stirrup pumps and the distance was short. But no! Down came an incendiary in the Archdeacon's Court and when this

who were dead or missing. Without warning, the King suddenly appeared in Army Uniform. He was walking with a group of people and I always remember a bus conductor who climbed a gas lamppost and clung on to it and waved his hat in the air and shouting, "Three cheers for King George." It was quite marvellous.

(*Below*) The shell of Owen Owen store stands on the right, while in the background the burnt out ruins of Coventry Market Hall stand. Below it (right) is the remains of West Orchard. Work is underway to clear the massive amount of rubble from the city which was used to infill field hollows both locally and throughout the county. Within three days the city had a fairly dependable bus service and within six weeks factories which were once targets, were almost back to full production. As the rubble was being cleared talk had already begun on rebuilding the city.

(*Below*) The blitz on Coventry had shocked the world for no English city had suffered such concentrated and prolonged bombing as on that fateful night. To add to the shock, Coventry's Cathedral of St. Michael also suffered and was the only English Cathedral to fall in the war. Photographs of the city and its devastated cathedral were shown everywhere causing worldwide

condemnation. On fire duty the night of its destruction were the Provost of St. Michael's, the Rev. Richard Howard, 'Jock' Forbes, the cathedrals stonemason, and Mr. White and Mr. Eaton. All had to protect the building with stirrup pumps, buckets of water and sand. At around 7.40pm on November 14th the cathedral was struck by its first incendiary; the fire brigade was immediately called. All four fought the flames as more fell burning through the lead roof; lead sheets had to be quickly lifted to extinguish the fires which were burning in the 18 inch inner roof space. As one string was dealt with another fell. Four landed on the east end burning through into the roof space of the Girdlers Chapel above the north door in the outer north aisle. The four firefighters rushed across the building and immediately set about trying to control the blaze which had by now grew considerably. With little equipment they fought a losing battle and soon the fire beat them back and began consuming the building. Knowing they could do no more, it was time to save what was portable from the building. Then the four went to the south porch and sat amid the explosions waiting for the fire brigade to arrive. At 9.30pm the Solihull Fire Brigade arrived and hoses were laid down around the cathedral to attack the seat of the fire. A hose was turned on and steam rose as the water hit the hot lead roof. Soon however the water stopped and it was quickly discovered that the mains had been hit; no more water was forthcoming. Meanwhile another fire, previously unnoticed, had taken hold of the nave and the south aisle. Here a policeman and soldier had climbed onto the roof and were throwing off what incendiaries they could; that was until the police officer was injured by an exploding incendiary – a device

which had seen its first use this night. By now the building was well ablaze and everyone continued salvaging what they could. By 10.30pm another hose was set up but once again the pressure was lost and all the firemen could do was to leave the cathedral to its fate. Later the Rev. Howard wrote: 'The whole interior

was a seething mass of flame with piled up blazing beams and timbers, interpenetrated and surmounted with dense bronze-coloured smoke.' Unexpectedly the main pillars in the cathedral one by one came crashing down, this was due to the fact that during the restoration in 1885-90 the main beams across the nave had been strengthened with steel strips. These strips expanded in the intense heat and, being riveted to the beams, caused them to twist and pull the main pillars inwards collapsing the interior of the building. While the Cathedral Church of St. Michael's blazed, the bells continued to chime the hours; many took this as a sign that the building lay untouched. Here we have the rubble filled ruin of the cathedral on the morning of the 15th. On the left, by the west door, can be seen the ladder which led onto the outer north aisle where the fatal fire first started. Little can be seen in the background for the city was held within a shroud of smoke. Provost Howard noted his thoughts after a visit to the ruined cathedral on this morning, he wrote: 'The heaped-up piles of rubble seemed to retain an immense degree of beauty as though they possessed something living and imperishable within themselves.' He later added, "We shall rebuild it to the glory of God."

(*Left*) Looking across the chancel towards the Lady Chapel. Underneath the rubble in the chapel lies buried the tomb of Bishop Yeatman-Biggs. It was soon dug out and found to be remarkably intact except for the bishops hands holding a model of St. Michael's which had been smashed off. Nothing else in the building survived. Much of the rubble in the central area has been cleared leaving the steel strips which were responsible for the collapse of the interior.

(*Left*) Looking down the nave and chancel through the North Porch; the huge medieval iron hinges hang motionless minus the great oak doors. Thousands of people wandered around amongst the ruins, as did the King who viewed the damage 24 hours after the raid. From the destruction arose the creation of the charred cross by the cathedral's stone mason 'Jock' Forbes. 'Jock' took two charred timbers from the rubble and bound them together with wire forming a cross which he planted where the alter once stood. Later this was placed on a simple stone alter called the 'Alter of Reconciliation,' and the Provost had the words 'Father Forgive' carved behind it. Another famous cross was created soon after by a local priest, the Rev. Wale who bound together three massive medieval iron nails forming what became internationally known as 'The Cross of Nails.' This was symbolic not only of the cathedral's destruction but also the suffering of Christ, the Trinity and the symbol of the worldwide Community of the Cross of Nails. Out of the destruction had been born a worldwide ministry of reconciliation and hope.

(*Right*) Destruction in Coventry did not end with the November blitz for the city was to continue suffering. Two particularly heavy raids on the 8th and 10th of April 1941 raised the death toll in the city to 1,200. Coventry endured 41 raids between 18th August 1940 and 3rd August 1942 and 373 siren alerts. This photograph taken on the 9th April 1941 shows what was, until the night before, the 17th century Grapes Inn which stood in Warwick Lane. It is said the inn was rebuilt timber by timber in the Civil War after it was moved from outside the city wall. Behind can be seen the burnt out shell of Christchurch which was destroyed by incendiaries. Soon, for the second time in its history, the church spire would stand alone as the main building was once again demolished.

TO CAR →

PARK

FRAME

CKETS ISSUED
HERE
FOR

L.M.S.
G.W.
..N.E.
OUTHERN
..WAYS.

RAILWAY BOOKIN

OFFICIAL STA

This photograph taken early in 1942, shows Broadgate and the central area clear of rubble. In the centre stands the Market Clock minus the market hall. The 100 foot high tower which had stood since 1867 was demolished in December 1942, one week after a boy was killed by falling masonry. Despite this, many believed the tower was still safe and should have remained. The clocks custodian, Samuel Corbett who had looked after it since 1892, died the night before its destruction unaware of what was to happen to his beloved timepiece. On the left of the tower is the line of Market Street leading to Smithford Street and on the right is West Orchard leading to the bottom of Smithford Street onto Fleet Street and St. John's. In the right background can be seen Leigh Mills in Hill Street, the gasometer and St. Osburgs. Note in the sky above the city can be seen a number of Barrage Balloons. These were scattered at sites around the city and occasionally fulfilled their purpose, although sometimes tragically as the Rev. Clitheroe of Holy Trinity recalled during August 1940. He wrote: 'I was alone at the Church and on the West roof, when a German plane struck one of barrage balloon cables, jettisoned its bombs on the houses of the Wallace Road area and killed and injured many of our citizens. The balloon drifted over the house tops and came down in Broadgate close to the church, where I helped to make it secure.'

Donald and the Rev. Kenneth Thornton; after Christmas 1940 the team was joined by Mr. Basil White. These men, with the aid of buckets, stirrup pumps, water and sand, took on the responsibility of keeping the nine roofs of Trinity free from incendiaries and stopped it sharing the same fate as St. Michael's. The Rev. Clitheroe wrote that the church was surrounded by fire and explosions and all had close calls as they dealt with incendiary fires both on and in the church and in the nearby Bell Tower. He later wrote, 'It was an incessant downpour of bombs and incendiaries and from the battlements the view might have been from Dante's *Inferno*. I could not believe then that anything had any chance of surviving.' The message on the church reflected the belief of the Rev. Clitheroe who said, "I was never prepared to face the possibility of losing Trinity while I could fight to save it." Note the air-raid shelter entrance in the middle of the picture, formed by covered sandbags.

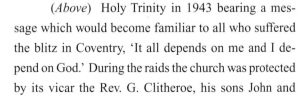

(*Above*) Holy Trinity in 1943 bearing a message which would become familiar to all who suffered the blitz in Coventry, 'It all depends on me and I depend on God.' During the raids the church was protected by its vicar the Rev. G. Clitheroe, his sons John and

(*Left*) Demolition underway of the first Owen Owen building in Trinity Street in August/September 1943. On the left is Broadgate and Hertford Street leading down to the spire of Christchurch. Above the air-raid shelter stands the Burton Building, behind which can be seen the Queen's Road Baptist Church and open countryside.

(*Right*) Demolition of Owen's from Cross Cheaping, showing the spires of Holy Trinity (left) and St. Michael's. On the right, above the fenced off area, is the entrance to West Orchard. The present Owen's stands on the upper part of the old site.

(*Below*) After Germany surrendered on Monday, May 7th 1945 and

with the official cessation of hostilities ending at one minute past midnight on the 8th, a two day holiday was held. The 8th was officially VE Day and crowds gathered in Broadgate to hear Winston Churchill's victory speech which was relayed live through loudspeakers. Throughout the city street parties took place and despite rationing great spreads of food were laid out. Here we see residents of Stevenson Road in Keresley enjoying their VE Day celebration. On the waste land behind them a bonfire with an effigy of Hitler hanging above awaits the night time festivities. The residents of Stevenson Road and many other suburbs of the city were not untouched by the city centre bombing. Many houses outside the centre of the city were destroyed by bombs including those which previously stood behind these revellers.

(*Right*)   Despite the cathedral's destruction the Provost, Rev. R.T. Howard, continued whenever possible to hold services in the ruins, the rubble serving as his pulpit. On VE Day thousands visited the cathedral and the Provost held short acts of prayer from 8am to midnight. At night the sanctuary was floodlit and a huge star of electric lights placed on the tower. It is said that tens of thousands came till 3am to stand silent in the ruins.

(*Below*)   Looking south up Broadgate and Hertford Street in 1946. Buses drop off their fares by the flower bed in Trinity Street as they do to this day. The waste ground, once the site of the shops, now bears nothing but grass and weeds. Talk in the Council House was of the resurrection of the city and plans, first submitted by City architect Donald Gibson in the beginning of 1941, were dusted off. Time for the modern phoenix to rise from the ashes of the old.

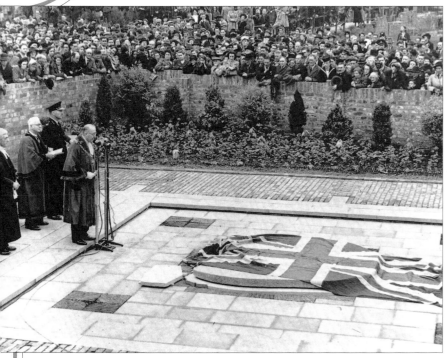

Cumberland granite. The two worked out the design between them and Tennant created the symbol of the 'Phoenix Rising.' Before a large crowd the stone was laid by the mayor Alderman George Briggs on Victory Day, 8th June 1946 on the site of the new precinct. In present terms the mayor would be standing by the entrance to Ernest Jones the jewellers under the ramp in the Upper Precinct.

(*Right*) The first area to be rebuilt was Broadgate Square where a garden island was created; this was officially opened by the then Princess Elizabeth in May 1948. In December of that year the Ministry of Works announced that one and a half million pounds had been allocated to the first stage of the city's rebuilding. On October 22nd 1949, Mrs Lewis Douglas, wife of the American Ambassador to the Court of St. James, unveiled the now famous bronze equestrian statue of Godiva entitled 'Self Sacrifice.' The £20,000 statue was the work of Sir William Reid Dick and was paid for by William Bassett-Green, the grandson of Eli Green a well known Coventry silk weaver. Note in the background, on the east-side of Broadgate, the temporary shops which survived into the sixties.

(*Above*) Before the war there were plans to rebuild parts of the city centre, including Smithford Street. After the November blitz a whole new world of possibilities opened up for redevelopment of the city, the destruction of the centre was a planners dream. In Coventry's case the dreamer was Donald Gibson who was appointed Coventry's first City Architect in 1938. Gibson envisaged the new city centre as a pedestrian area bordered on the north with parkland on which stood places of cultural interest. The latter part of his plan never came to fruition, except for the building of the Belgrade Theatre, but the precinct, the first in Britain, was laid out much to his original design. After the council had successfully acquired the land, the first act of rebuilding was the laying of the Phoenix levelling stone. Gibson was given permission to acquire the stone and with his friend, artist Trevor Tennant, drove to the Lake District where they chose a suitable piece of

(*Right*) Part of the new centre, nothing more than a building site, something the citizens of Coventry would have to get used to for many years to come. Unlike the old Coventry the new would be made of steel and concrete. The upper section of Smithford Street was closed to traffic in January 1948 and demolition contractors moved into the Burton Building, followed by Wilsons, then the Savings Centre. On the north side of the street, while demolishing Weaver to Wearer, workman uncovered an ancient wall made of massive blocks of sandstone – this was covered up again. The first building to be completed was Broadgate House opened by Lord Silkin in May 1953.

(*Below*) Broadgate in July 1954. The £940,000 Owen Owen building is still unfinished as the Hotel Leofric rises next door. It was designed by Hattrell &

Partners with the intention of mirroring Gibson's Broadgate House.

(*Right*) Godiva stands on her garden island and behind her the newly completed Owen Owen building which was opened by the Lord Mayor, Ald. John Fennell on 1st October 1954. The building was designed by Hellberg and Harris who, like all outside architects, followed the Councils requirements concerning the height and general design of the buildings. On the left the Hotel Leofric is still under construction.

(*Right*) The developers of the Hotel Leofric put forward a proposal to finish the Upper Precinct which was at first refused by the council but later accepted during February 1953. Gibson based the concept of the two tier design of the Upper Precinct on the Rows of Chester and the brickwork was chosen to blend in with an important focal point, the tower and spire of St. Michael's. Note in the photograph the elephant and castle; the mast was made by Armstrong Whitworth and the gilded elephant and castle came out of the workshops of Motor Panels. This was erected to mark the site of the Savings for Reconstruction Exhibition held nearby in March 1948. It also served the dual purpose of marking the uppermost point of the Upper Precinct.

(*Below*) Looking down the Upper Precinct along the original Smithford Street in 1954. This photograph was taken by Trevor Pring from the unfinished balcony of the south-side of the precinct. On the right can be seen the White Lion Public House and Restaurant still *in situ* in Smithford Street. This was the second inn on the site, the previous building dating from at least the 18th century. The inn gained some notoriety in 1734 when Thomas Wildley murdered his aunt Sussanah Wall, and her daughter Ann Shenton who kept the inn. Marks and Spencer, below the White Lion, was opened in April 1954, while work was also well underway on British Home Stores on the left. In the background, still open to traffic, is the lower part of Smithford Street leading to Fleet Street and St. John's.

(*Above*) Late in 1954 and the work continues apace. The gents toilet can be seen in the foreground and next to Marks and Spencer work has begun on the pedestrian bridge. Notice that the White Lion has been replaced.

(*Below*) The bridge and connecting stairs is now half complete, as is much of the paving of the Upper Precinct now decorated with cherry trees. Hundreds of people wander past still making use of surviving and temporary shops scattered around the centre.

(*Below*) July 1955 nearly there! Donald Gibson's plan draws to a conclusion. He was not however here to see it for in the January of that year he left Coventry to become Director General of Works at the War Office. He was replaced by Arthur Ling who continued work on extending the precinct.

(*Right*) Late autumn 1955 and the Upper Precinct is finally completed and fully open to the public. The precinct was built in what became known as 'Festival of Britain' style.

(*Above*) Early 1955 and the Upper precinct is nearing completion. Opposite Marks and Spencer stands British Home Stores which was built at a cost of £400,000 and opened on May 20th 1955. Below that can be seen the second store built (the first was Home and Fashion in Broadgate House), namely the Woolworth's store which opened in August 1953. This store stretched along the whole length of Market Way which, under Gibson's plan, was to remain a road open to traffic. The toilets in the Upper Precinct were built in what was a static water tank used during the war.

Looking across Broadgate and down the Precinct from St. Michael's in 1955. Broadgate House, on the left, officially opened in May 1953 although the first of its lower shops opened earlier in March. Also that year, a department store opened within the building called Home and Fashion. This store traded until 1960 when it was taken over by The Coventry Cash Stores. The store took up three floors, the first was household goods, linens and fabric; the second, electrical goods, hardware and furniture and on the third floor a supermarket. The 'Cash Store' only traded until August 1961 and much of the building lay empty until 1963 when the upper floors were converted to offices. To the left of Broadgate House and spanning Hertford Street is the Bridge Restaurant. This Restaurant lasted into the late 1960's when the street was pedestrianised. Gibson's original plan of an upper and lower precinct included a road running through what is now Market Way and Smithford Way. Construction of the road was started and until recently could be seen between Woolworths and British Home Stores in Market Way. When Ling began work he rightly put an end to this idea despite opposition from local tradespeople. Note in the background the bottom of Smithford Street still remains intact.

(*Below*) Barretts Shoes of Northampton and E. Palmer, Pork Butcher stand empty *in situ* on Smithford Street next to the side of Marks and Spencer. Behind them stands Smithford Way, half built and half blocked by older properties.

(*Below Left*) Further down, below Barretts, stands the bottom floor of the old Co-op building. Once an impressive store it lost its upper floors during the blitz. The last shop to trade in Smithford Street was Marlows Furniture and Radio shop which was closed on the 4th May 1957. Before the war the shop was a pub called the Empire Vaults.

(*Below*) Further down and on the corner of West Orchard and Fleet Street stands the City Arms. Opposite, on the corner of Smithford Street, stands the Co-op as seen in the previous photograph and behind stands St. John's. After the late Victorian City Arms was demolished to make way for the lower Precinct it reopened in Smithford Way and in recent years this too has been demolished.

(*Above*) Newly opened Smithford Way still remains unconnected with the Precinct and Corporation Street as shops still partially block the way. On display is the city's plan for the rebuilding of the city centre. This was originally the path of Gibson's road which was to bisect the precinct and was altered by Arthur Ling. The Upper Precinct, including Market Way and Smithford Way, was finally completed in 1955 and contained 88 shops, 3 large stores and 1 pub – the rebuilt City Arms.

(*Right*) The bottom half of Smithford Street and Fleet Street was finally closed in July 1958 and clearance work began for the start of the Lower Precinct designed by city architect Arthur Ling. Gibson's two tier shopping in the Upper Precinct never quite took off simply because people were not inclined to climb the stairs, so Ling designed the Lower Precinct to be more compact and more easily accessible. Here we see Land Gear of Birmingham unloading a digger at the bottom of West Orchard as work begins on the Lower Precinct. The scaffolding in the background has no connection with the building work as it was left standing from before 1942; probably a building unfinished due to the war. In the background can be seen the spire of St. Osburg's at the top of Hill Street.

(*Right*) July/August 1958 and work has begun on culverting the Sherbourne which ran directly across the site of the Lower Precinct. Interestingly this later development proved relevant in 1994 when a scheme was put forward to move the market into the Lower Precinct. After much opposition to moving the market together with traders wanting a higher roof level, the developers pulled out after discovering difficulties lowering the floor level created by the river culvert. Sadly and ironically this scheme was opposed *en-masse* because of re-siting the market. This was despite the

fact that the plan, designed by local architects Corstorphine & Wright of Warwick, would have rebuilt a new High Street together with connecting roads. Building designs included period style reconstructions of old Coventry dwellings covering a 400 year history of the city. For the first time since the blitz Coventry had a chance to regain some of the style it had lost but it was left to slip away. This photograph was taken in West Orchard, in the background can be seen the City Arms.

The temporary shops built on the east-side of blitzed Broadgate and officially opened on December 3rd 1947. Many will remember these shops as they were a dropping off point for a number of buses in Broadgate. Many will also remember the café which took the space used in this photograph by Spalls the giftware shop which moved to the top of the Lower Precinct. Running along the back of these buildings was Derby Lane, now like the rest of this site under Cathedral Lanes. This was a medieval lane dating back to at least 1327. When these shops were demolished for landscaping in the 1970's the area was excavated and found to contain numerous medieval houses and workshops. Underneath the site of Spalls a well was uncovered; this was capped and used as a wishing well in the later landscaping scene. Behind the temporary buildings can be seen (left) the Central Library and the City Council Staff Canteen. On the far right, attached to what was Atkins & Turton, is Martin's Bank and lastly the Coventry Building Society. The tall and rather oddly shaped building on the right appears almost like an optical illusion, looking as if it were flat.

The south-west corner of Broadgate in 1960. In the background is Broadgate House occupied by a three storied department store, Coventry Cash Stores. The lower shops included Kendall's and Hepworth's. Behind Devlins is the Bridge Restaurant opened on 1st January 1955. This high class restaurant seated 172 and because of its good food and notable view, was well patronised for 26 years until its closure in October 1981. Hertford Street carried traffic under the restaurant until the road was closed and pedestrianised in 1969. The Hertford Street subway in the centre of the picture (begun 1949) was one of two subways in Broadgate. It took pedestrians under Hertford Street, while a second ran 100 feet across Trinity Street.

Looking down the Precinct in the late 1960's. The Cash Stores in Broadgate House is now gone and the building has been converted into offices. The Leofric Hotel was in the fifties and sixties the most heavily booked hotel outside London. When it first opened the hotel charged 37 shillings and 6 pence a night with breakfast and the penthouse suite, used by entertainers from Gracie Fields to Mick Jagger, was 120 shillings a night. At the bottom of the Precinct stands Mercia House, a tall building containing a Restaurant, night club and flats. This was designed principally by J. M. McLellan under the direction of Arthur Ling who, unlike Gibson, believed the centre needed tall buildings to add to the skyline ending the dominance of the three spires. In the background (left) can be seen the G.E.C. factory which began life as Rudge Cycles. This was one of the factories that made Coventry the largest producer of cycles in the world. The factory was demolished in recent years to become the home of a new complex called the Motor Plaza 100 a celebration of the centenary of the motor car whose birthplace was Coventry.

The bottom of Trinity Street in the early 1950's. Beyond the traffic island stands the Hippodrome and behind that Swanswell Gate and Lady Herbert's Garden. Behind the garden, part of the old Chauntry still stands. Across the bottom of Trinity Street the Sherbourne once flowed and fed a watermill behind the building on the left. The river is now culverted.

Broadgate Island in the early 1950's. The island opened in 1948 contained hundreds of plants and bulbs supplied by the citizens of Holland in gratitude for their liberation by the Allies during World War II. On the left stands an empty space where Owen and Owen would be rebuilt.

NEW LIFE AFTER SACRIFICE

The rebuilding of the city centre was of great importance to post war planners. It pioneered new regions but did not catch the imagination of the world like the building of the new Cathedral of St. Michael. The Provost the Very Reverend R.T. Howard wrote in his book *Ruined and Rebuilt* that as he went into the ruined cathedral the morning after its destruction, 'there flashed into my mind the deep certainty that as the Cathedral had been crucified with Christ, so it would rise again with Him. How or when, we could not tell; nor did it matter. THE CATHEDRAL WOULD RISE AGAIN....' Within the year the Cathedral Council met to discuss the rebuilding on or near the site of the ruins. Sir Giles Gibert Scott, the designer of Liverpool's new cathedral, was invited to submit a new design. His proposal, built on the site of the old and with a central alter, was approved by the Cathedral Council but the Royal Fine Arts Commission thought otherwise and Sir Giles withdrew his plan. It was not until 1950 that the Council held an open competition; the result was that they received 219 entries from all over the world, many of which proposed the total destruction of the old Cathedral. The winning entry, announced in August 1951, was tendered by Basil Spence (later knighted for this work), Spence had always dreamed of building a cathedral and in October 1950 had visited the ruins of St. Michael and within the first five minutes a vision of the new came to him. He later said of this visit that he was in a 'high state of ecstasy' as the ruins seemed to say "I am the sacrifice; build now for the new life, the resurrection." With tears in his eyes he saw through a shattered north window, "the new Cathedral growing out of the old." At the end, "a great tapestry of the risen Christ, large and triumphant, and through a great glass screen with figures of saints and martyrs I saw the new nave." When Spence's new design was revealed by the press there was no perspective view available only ground plans which did not receive a welcome and were blasted by many as a 'monstrosity.' Spence rode a storm of disapproval and received over 700 letters opposing his plans; of these he said, "Eighty per cent were very, very rude and the remaining twenty percent of them were rude." Spence's dream nearly turned into a nightmare when due to this controversy commissions started to dry up and his practice received no work for nearly two years, bringing him to the verge of bankruptcy. This would all quickly change as his name grew with his cathedral. In 1954 the Ministry of Works gave permission to build the new Cathedral of St. Michael and Sir David Eccles, the Minister who granted permission, added 'The Cathedral is not a building which concerns Coventry alone. The echo of the bombs which destroyed your city was heard round the world. We cannot tell how many people are waiting in this country and abroad for this church to rise and prove that English traditions live again after the blitz.'

(*Centre*) Coventry Cathedral ruins in 1949 was still regularly used for services and ceremonial purposes while waiting for the new Cathedral to be built. In the aspe can be seen the original charred cross on the stone alter and behind the words 'Father Forgive.' To its left can be seen the Lady Chapel with the tomb of Bishop Yeatman-Biggs in its new position and the Hood memorial still *in situ*. The third window down in the chapel was soon to become an arch connecting the old to the new and is named the 'Queen's Way' after its use by Queen Elizabeth II when the new building was consecrated. The rubble which had lined the edges of the building since 1940 was removed in 1948 and parts of the ruins were grassed. Note the concentration of buildings in the background, most of which were demolished for building Coventry University.

Row was closed on March 7th 1955 and demolition work took place to extend the site. Deep excavation of the site for the undercroft revealed that much of the ground had been made-up some time in the distant past. The east end of the old Priory was unearthed as was a wall of the Bishops Palace and many carved and decorated stones were unearthed. In one corner of the site spools of silk were discovered and pieces of equipment used for its production; this was thought to date back nearly 200 years. Laying the foundations was begun by Laing Construction in March 1955. Sir John Laing thought this to be his companies greatest work and used only his best men under instruction that the building should be built like the cathedral's of old, to last a thousand years.

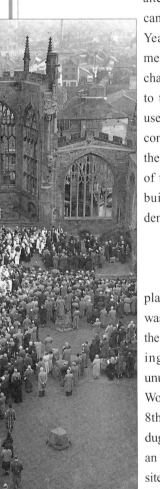

(*Right*) Basil Spence's plan for the new Cathedral was to attach it to the ruins of the old by a porch. The building was centred on an unusual north to south basis. Work officially began on June 8th 1954 when a workman dug a sod for the erection of an oak fence to enclose the site. As this area consisted of the old St. Michael's graveyard, many hundreds of skeletons from many centuries had to be disinterred; this was slow work and lasted through much of 1954. Priory

April 1955 the old Cathedral stands empty as work continues on the new. Note the ruins have been tidied up some years earlier with the removal of loose pinnacles and the sealing of some of the walls to make them water proof. On the site, Laing's began laying the first of 670 piles for the walls. These piles were two feet apart and created by making bore holes 14 inches across and up to 30 feet deep down to bedrock. In the holes were inserted steel rods and concrete. Note New Street running off in the background, tradition has it that this street was built and occupied by the original builders of the first St. Michael's in the 14th century and indeed, hidden under this brickwork, were timbered buildings. This however did not stop their demolition in the early 1960's. The building obscured by the tree was thought to have began life as the medieval 'Chapel of the Cross.'

(*Below*) The undercroft externally nears completion during the late summer of 1957. Designed as a large storage area, the undercroft was adapted as the 'Chapel of the Cross' and was used for services for nearly four years while the cathedral grew overhead. When the cathedral opened, the undercroft was divided into smaller areas and used as a vestry, social centre, library and BBC television studio. Behind can be seen Priory Street and the Victorian building occupied by Triumph.

(*Above*) Looking northwest across the site in April 1955. Behind this scraped piece of Coventry soil was a mass of activity as the best British and foreign artists were being engaged to create one of the greatest buildings of the 20th century. For the new Cathedral was to be as much a work of art as it was to be a building. At the rear of the site can be seen the extension to the Triumph factory and beyond that lies Pool Meadow. Two hundred years earlier most of this area was still well wooded and led down to the pool known as the Mill Dam.

(*Left*) Photographed from the tower of the old Cathedral in early 1957 the new Cathedral is taking shape. The zig-zag line of the walls is now discernable as is the Chapel of Unity alongside. One can only now appreciate the scale of the building when compared to the figures standing inside it. The three feet thick walls were built like 'massive cliffs' and alternated with windows running the whole length of the building. The only exception was for where the great east window, the Baptistery Window' designed by John Piper dominates. The walls were built so that from the south their line is broken by windows, but from the north the wall appears as one solid mass, a solidity which was inspired by Norman Cathedral's such as Durham. Note in the background, to the right of the Triumph Works, stands the entrance to Cope Street one of Coventry's many lost streets.

(*Right*) The foundation stone was laid in 1956 and on May 25th 1962 the new Cathedral of St. Michael, which cost £1,250,000, was consecrated. The Queen led the ceremony before hundreds of bishops and clergy from around the world who were seated amongst the 2,300 people that filled the building – outside in the ruins of the old Cathedral sat a further 2,000. That day the world's eyes were on Coventry. Here we see the nave which measures some 270 feet long and 800 feet wide. The 14th century style vaulting grows from slender pillars which taper inwards as they descend. The interior lining of the wall was done single-handedly by one man, Eric Macleod. On these walls are eight stone tablets carved by Ralph Beyer and bearing passages from the Scriptures reflecting the life of Christ. The nave culminates with the High Alter which stands before what was until fairly recently the largest tapestry in the world. Designed by Graham Sutherland the tapestry entitled

'Christ in Glory in the Tetramorph' covers the ecclesiastical east (geographically the north) wall to a height of nearly 75 feet. The tapestry was produced in France over a two year period on a 500 year old loom and used 12000 miles of wool. It was paid for by an anonymous city benefactor who gave £20,000. The Cathedral also holds many other great works such as Jacob Epstein's 'St. Michael and the Devil' his last major work which was unveiled posthumously by his wife. The beautiful baptistry window designed by John Piper and executed by Patrick Reyntiens. John Hutton's spectacular west screen decorated with saints and angels graven into the glass and constitutes the largest glass screen in the world. Inside this screen set into the floor in huge brass letters is this inscription by Ralph Beyer, it reads: 'TO THE GLORY OF GOD * THIS CATHEDRAL BURNT NOVEMBER 14 AD 1940 IS NOW REBUILT * 1962'.

(Below) Hales Street photographed on the 16th March 1951. The war had been over for nearly six years yet the upper windows of H. Evans & Son are still taped up to protect against bomb blast. Opposite stands the Opera House which was the thriving home of the Coventry Repertory Company until the stage was destroyed by bomb damage in 1940. The Opera House was well supported and theatre goers enjoyed the music of the Noel Wimperis Orchestra before curtain up and during the intervals. The bar was well used and the theatre had its own extended social circle of over 1000 members, many of whom would visit the West End regularly on trains run specially for the Repertory Company.

(*Below*) A much changed view of Greyfriars Green photographed around 1952. Standing prominently in the foreground is the statue of city benefactor Sir Thomas White erected in 1882. Not a Coventrian

but born in Reading in 1492, Thomas White made his fortune in London as a merchant. He was later knighted and served as the city's Lord Mayor. He founded his charity in 1542 with a gift of £1,400 given to Coventry Corporation's charity administrator to buy back land confiscated by the Crown during the Dissolution. Other places to benefit from his charity were Warwick, Leicester, Northampton and Nottingham. At its initial conception the charity was to pay out £70 a year with £10 given on loan to four apprentices for nine years and £2 a year to twelve poor men. Others to benefit were the mayor, recorder, ten aldermen, the town clerk of Coventry and the London Taylors Company. With the charities acquisition of land, its yearly income has grown considerably since its foundation to £40,000 a year and each town mentioned previously shares this windfall in rotation. Behind the statue across a rather flat Greyfriars Green, can be seen Victorian Stoneleigh Terrace on Queen's Road which was demolished in the 1960's to build the Ring-road.

(*Centre*) Warwick Row in the mid 1950's. During this period the road was still open to through traffic linking Queen's Road with Hertford Street. On the right is Greyfriars Green, the Thomas White statue, and beyond the spire of Christchurch. The last building on the left is Loviett's estate agents, previously known as Nantglyn.

The building still standing today was the school of the Franklin sisters early in the 19th century. Here between 1832-5 was educated Mary Ann Evans, better known to the world as the novelist George Eliot. The Franklin sisters, Rebecca and Mary were the daughters of the Rev. Francis Franklin the minister of Cow Lane Chapel. Both had a great influence on the young Mary Ann in religious ideas and personal appearance and speech; in the latter Mary Ann was much influenced by Miss Rebecca who had acquired 'Parisian' manners while abroad. It is said that Mary Ann's desk was near the back door of the building and she would often stare out mesmerised across the open fields. She returned to live in Coventry six years later and on this occasion met Charles Bray of Rosehill, in Radford. Bray, a noted 'freethinker' in the city, had great influence on the growing Mary Ann and turned her mind from religion to writing, publishing her first works anonymously in the Coventry Herald which he then owned. Through him she met many notables of the period and grew from a simple country girl to an intelligent, confident woman. Mary Ann Evans may have been born in Nuneaton, but George Eliot, the writer was truly born in Coventry.

(*Below*) Late 18th century workers cottages lie empty in Whitefriars Lane in 1955. At the end of the lane in Gosford Street stand buildings dating back to at least the 16th century. Buildings of this style were once

fairly common in the city and now the only survivors stand at the top of Hill Street. When restored they make rather attractive buildings but who then thought to restore the common dwelling house.

While dwelling houses were being demolished in the city centre new ones were being built on the outskirts. Here we see flats being erected in Tile Hill during 1955-6. In the background the buildings appear to have no particular plan in this hotchpotch development. The Tile Hill Estate did however win a Government award for its layout and was for many years considered the city's premiere estate. So happy was the city with Wimpey's fast work in erecting the estate that one road was named after the supervisor of the construction team; that road was Jardine Crescent. Notice how Tile Hill Wood dominates the background, looking almost like a forest.

(*Right*) The bottom of Hertford Street and the Bull Yard around 1960. Tom still peeps from his fourth floor window of the former Peeping Tom Inn which is now G. E. Jones who advertise themselves as 'The Famous Clothers.' Above the Hillman Minx and Jaguar, stands the well known Geisha Café which occupied these premises for nearly 60 years until its closure in 1961. After it closed, its well-liked staff all found employ with Gladding's in the new Shelton Square. An interesting fact during this period, when the car industry began to boom was that Coventrians had more cars per person than anywhere else in the land. Also 75 per cent of Coventrians were not born in the City!

(*Right*) The top of Hertford Street in the early 1960's. Many will remember the Empire Cinema which began life in the 19th century as the Corn Exchange. The upper frontage belongs to the original façade. Much of Hertford Street was destroyed in the various bombings and many companies continued in ground level and temporary shops. All of the west side of the street was demolished when the area was made into a pedestrian precinct which was finally completed in 1972. Behind the Empire can be seen the Barracks car park built on the site of the old Coventry Barracks which opened in 1793.

(*Below*) In this photograph taken in Hales Street looking down White Street, we see reflections of the past and present. In the foreground workmen are digging up the cobbled road and tram tracks which carried trams to Stoke and Bell Green from 1899 to 1940. The line going to the right ran into Ford Street and further down on the left they also entered Jesson Street. The plan for these tracks was first proposed to Parliament in 1897 and when permission was granted, laid down by the Coventry Electric Tramways Company. In the background we see the modern face of Coventry, the Inner Ring Road under construction, a concept first mooted in the 1930's. The ring road was included in Gibson's plan for the redevelopment of the city and was begun in 1958 from London Road to Quinton Road (opened 1959) and slowly encircled the city over 12 years until it was finally finished.

(*Above*) Broadgate in the mid–1960's. Godiva looking much darker than she is now sits proudly on her horse, open to the sky and the central figure in Broadgate. She looks south towards the Godiva Clock which has just struck ten. The figures of Godiva and Peeping Tom caused much controversy when first unveiled to the public, many considered them too much like fairground carvings and beneath the dignity of the legendary Lady. The sculptures were made by Trevor Tennant, who also carved the Phoenix Stone, and despite being disliked by some Coventrians they soon

became very popular with tourist as they are to this day. The clock was originally electric, but being unreliable was replaced with the old market clock mechanism made by Coventry clockmaker Edward Loseby in 1870. The bell attached to the side of the tower originally rang on the hour, every hour. This was soon stopped when guests at the Leofric complained that it kept them awake at night.

(*Above*) This beautiful Christmas photograph taken by Trevor Pring shows another view of Broadgate looking to the north at the Owen Owen Department Store. Godiva stands floodlit and accompanied by two fine Christmas trees. Owen's had its own spectacular Santa's Grotto with the annual line of fidgety children and anxious parents waiting outside.

(*Right*) The centre of Coventry occasionally suffered floods as did some of the surrounding districts. Here we see the Radford Road, alongside Radford Common, after the Radford Brook had burst its banks. On the right stands two rows of early 19th century cottages; the first is Summer Row and the second, which may have had top-shops at the rear, is Bambury's Buildings. They were built on land which was once the site of the medieval Radford Cross and the common opposite has been common land for a thousand years. Paddy Gill, the once famed Coventry prize fighter, had his first match on the common in 1838. Much of the old Radford village survived into this century but sadly much, including Summer Row and Bambury's Buildings, were demolished in the 1960's.

(*Left*) The demolition of shops is underway on the 19th April 1966 at the bottom of Warwick Lane as work begins on New Union Street. The Central Hall lies fully exposed as the shops, which survived the blitz, are finally demolished. At the junction with Hertford Street, Greens the Chemist still stands which was to occupy the shop into the 1980's. The Peeping Tom pub on the left has now disappeared as the west side of Hertford Street was rebuilt. The road is still open to traffic and will be for another three years.

Coventry had its carnival's, its fairs and Godiva Processions. Here we have the 'Festival of Britain' Godiva Pageant in 1951 with 28 year old London student and actress Ann Wrigg as Godiva. It is remembered that Ann Wrigg was an excellent Godiva despite the fact that her horse, Willoughby Warrior was not himself that day and caused many anxious moments with his restlessness. This photograph was taken in Jordan Well from the canopy of the cinema and the row of Elizabethan buildings behind the crowds were unceremonious torn down in the 1960's to open up the view of the Herbert Art Gallery and Museum which had been built behind them.

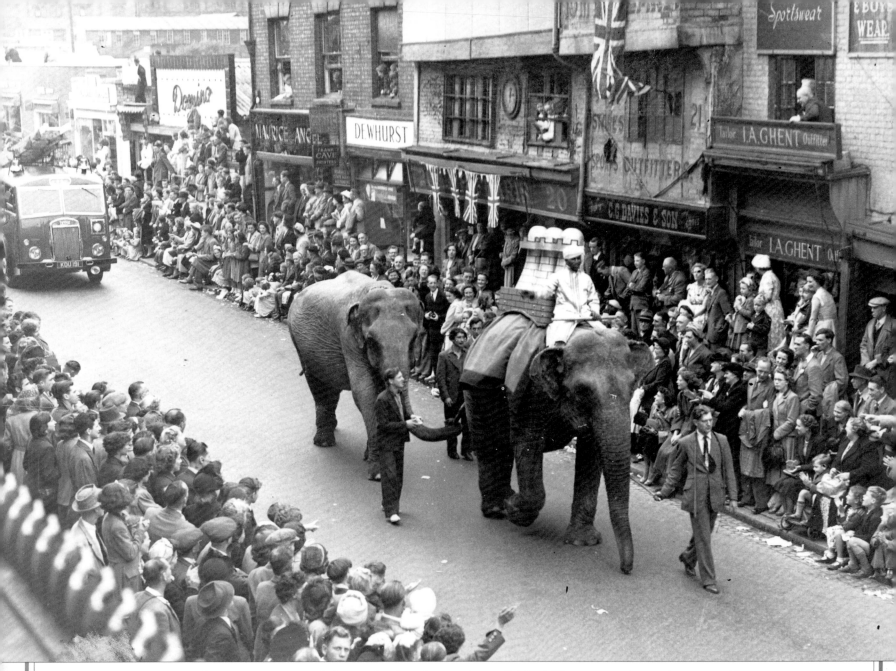

There was some speculation at the time that Godiva's horse may have been restless because of these elephants coming up behind. Their names were Salt and Sauce; one of them had to be the elephant from Coventry's city arms in the pageant, but one was not happy without the other so both came, one holding the others tail. The 1951 pageant was a major event with sixty tableaux's representing historical and industrial themes. For authenticity the organiser of the pageant obtained 1,500 period costumes from London. The five mile long pageant wove through the city streets and was remembered as being amongst the finest ever held.

(*Below*) The Coventry Carnival of 1955 started as always from the Memorial Park. Here we have Binley Wood Social Club's tableaux passing the old Styvechale toll-house on the Leamington Road.

(*Right*) A rather unusual Coventry built Daimler. Converted by Bass Brewery as an advertising gimmick it prepares to leave the Memorial Park. The vehicle is now in the Bass Museum at Burton upon Trent. Behind it stands the tableaux of the Dunlop Works, Holbrook Lane. All the city's major companies contributed to the success of the carnivals.

(*Right*) During the carnival and throughout the evening the Great Fair was held in the Memorial Park. This photograph by Cliff Barlow was taken on the 18th June 1955 and shows a bustling fair.

(*Above*) A corner of the Great Fair and a stall bearing the name Lt. Commander Ian Fraser VC, DSC, which claims to show 'Actual Wartime Operations Re-enacted.' The re-enactment was performed, with permission of the Admiralty, by frogmen in a 2000 gallon tank and compared by Freddie Baldwin DSM, late of H.M Submarines.

(*Centre*) A later carnival from the 1960's photographed as the Carnival Queen passes in front of Holy Trinity Church. Coventry city centre was packed on such days with people taking every vantage point possible, the procession went on and on as Coventry firms from the largest to smallest ran their own floats and bands played as they marched the streets. This was very much a community event making all aware that they were part of a prosperous industrial city. Note the steeple jacks on top of the spire of St. Michael's.

(*Below*) Not all parades were as huge as the old Coventry Carnival parades, here we see the Campfire Girls marching on a Sunday.

Part of the same parade marching along Ford Street past the Elastic Inn and the Alexandra Cinema. The Alexandra was the first cinema in the city to show a talkie, namely the *Jazz Singer* with Al Jolson shown in April 1929. It became the Theatre One in 1970.

INDEX